Terrorism

Terrorism

The Present Threat in Context

Stephen Sloan

**With a Foreword by John C. Bersia
and an Appendix by J. B. Hill and Joshua A. Smith**

Oxford • New York

English edition
First published in 2006 by
Berg
Editorial offices:
First Floor, Angel Court, 81 St Clements Street, Oxford OX4 1AW, UK
175 Fifth Avenue, New York, NY 10010, USA

Berg is the imprint of Oxford International Publishers Ltd.

Library of Congress Cataloging-in-Publication Data
Sloan, Stephen, 1936-
Terrorism : the present threat in context / Stephen
Sloan ; with a foreword by John C. Bersia and an
appendix by J. B. Hill and Joshua A. Smith.—English
ed.

p. cm.
Includes bibliographical references and index.
ISBN-13: 978-1-84520-344-3 (pbk.)
ISBN-10: 1-84520-344-5 (pbk.)
ISBN-13: 978-1-84520-343-6 (cloth)
ISBN-10: 1-84520-343-7 (cloth)
1. Terrorism. I. Title.

HV6431.S565 2006
363.325—dc22   2006017676

British Library Cataloguing-in-Publication Data
A catalogue record for this book is available from the British Library.

ISBN-13   978 1 84520 343 6 (Cloth)
          978 1 84520 344 3 (Paper)

ISBN-10   1 84520 343 7 (Cloth)
          1 84520 344 5 (Paper)

Typeset by Avocet Typeset, Chilton, Aylesbury, Bucks
Printed in the United Kingdom by Biddles Ltd, King's Lynn.

www.bergpublishers.com

Dedicated to Chris, Greg and Maya Sloan

Contents

Foreword

In the early 1990s, while researching issues related to aviation security for a journalistic project, I spoke with several colleagues who praised the work of a scholar I knew by reputation but had never met: Stephen Sloan, then of the University of Oklahoma.

Sloan had co-authored a book titled *Corporate Aviation Security* and it appeared he could add a valuable dimension to my research. Since my practice also was to seek to expand my database of sources, I telephoned Sloan, although not without cautioning myself that he might be too busy to bother. As circumstances turned out, he was available, charming, brimming with information and absolutely willing to continue the conversation beyond the immediate topic. In other words, he had the makings of the consummate source.

Of course, I did not let on at the time that he appeared to be as ideal a purveyor of balanced information and perspective on terrorism issues as a journalist might hope to find, but my guess is he understood me as well as I understood him before our first discussion had run its course. Most valuable to me was that Sloan sought to place the various terrorism topics that entered our conversations into appropriate contexts, similar to what he does in this book. Terrorism and counter-terrorism perspectives without contexts are like meals without spices and condiments; although blandly filling, they leave one far less than satisfied and inspired than otherwise might be the case.

Sloan entered my professional life at a particularly opportune time. I had just completed several years of covering political violence and terrorism in Europe, North Africa and the Middle East and I was embroiled in a challenging task that remains unfinished to this day: unraveling the complexities of the evolving terrorism phenomenon that began to metamorphose in increasingly unpredictable directions after the end of the Cold War.

Like Sloan, I had cut my teeth on the global framework imposed by the East–West divide and had come to view the world through a prism of black, white and a fair bit of gray. Yet I understood all along that the international order of the contending superpowers was ultimately ephemeral. Should one titan falter, the global structure quickly would change, as indeed it did after 1991 and the gray areas would proliferate.

Had the general population paid attention at that juncture, it would have realized that the historical forces the Cold War had artificially controlled – including terrorism – soon would rumble, rear their ugly heads and multiply with unpredictable persistence.

I thought about that potential problem as I discussed with Sloan aviation security weaknesses at that time and he shared with me an idea he and other scholars had contemplated with more than a bit of concern – that of the possible use of aircraft as weapons, directed into buildings with the impact and ferocity of bombs. I recalled that image as I read Sloan's line in this book's chapter on the future of terrorism. "Predicting the future is perhaps best left to seers," he wrote. Quite right, because no one can say with certainty what will transpire beyond today. But those with special insight can offer informed projections about what could happen and in that regard Sloan has turned in a stellar performance more often than I can count.

His concept of terrorists' using aircraft essentially as guided missiles carried me far beyond the aircraft-hijacking mindset which, along with random attacks at airports, had dominated my concepts of aviation-related terrorism. But I and probably most others who heard similar versions shelved that provocative thought until a day a decade later, on 9/11, when Sloan's prescient assessment came to haunt me, as it does to this day.

Over the years, Sloan provided invaluable perspectives during several other moments of terrorist-induced crisis – the first World Trade Center bombing in 1993; the Algeria-connected attacks in France during the mid-1990s; the bombings of US embassies in sub-Saharan Africa in 1998; attacks in Bali in 2002 and 2005; bombings in Casablanca, Riyadh and Istanbul in 2003; the

Madrid attacks of 2004; and the London subway bombings of 2005.

The most vivid recollection I have, though, is of the 1995 bombing of the Alfred P. Murrah Federal Building in Oklahoma City. Sloan was among the initial non-emergency eyewitnesses on the scene that fateful day in April. I know because I was facing an early deadline, as well as the need to find a specialist who could provide informed speculation about the attack. As I telephoned Sloan, who then lived mere blocks from the scene, he calmly indicated he was on his way and would arrive within minutes. He then proceeded to use his prodigious experience and expertise to comment on the situation. Most importantly, he was the first person to my knowledge who stepped back from the tragedy and advised against jumping to the conclusion that a person of Middle Eastern origin necessarily perpetrated the crime. As Americans later learned, the attack was home-grown.

Counter-terrorism studies evolved rapidly during the post-Cold War period and continue to change at a hectic pace, mirroring the quickly mutating terrorism phenomenon. Therefore, I particularly value having access to Sloan's wisdom and insight on a daily basis; he joined the staff of the University of Central Florida as a Fellow and University Professor in 2004.

That was a notable time in the University's history; it had embarked on an institution-changing quest just three years before. The University's goal was no less than to create an environment so hospitable to inquiry into global issues that it would reshape the academic and co-curricular environment over the course of five years. UCF's date with global destiny came a bit early. As Sloan arrived and began his work, evidence was mounting that the accelerated internationalization effort was succeeding. The five-year plan was completed at the end of year three. Sloan's arrival, which precipitated a growing focus on terrorism and political violence, also helped shape a new five-year strategic cycle.

We are slightly more than a year into that process at the moment and it brings me no pleasure to note that political violence dominates a disproportionate share of our work. If I could will it all away, I would in an instant. But that is not the nature of modern society. Our current lot is to live with the terrorism burden and our charge to stay at least far enough ahead of its relentless churning to prevent the erosion of our way of life. Terrorists, in addition to disrupting the status quo, can provoke otherwise rational leaders to push the pendulum in an extreme direction, eroding civil rights to the point that they risk joining terrorists in afflicting the masses. Maintaining the proper balance between national security and the protection of our founding principles is absolutely vital.

With that idea in mind, I will say unequivocally that the war against terrorism should have been launched when I first met Sloan, if not before. It is, therefore, a shortcoming that all modern US presidents share. President George W. Bush, to his credit, saw 9/11 with a sense of clarity that US commanders-in-chief rarely muster.

During an intense discussion in 2000, shortly before Bush took office, I quizzed him about several of the foreign-policy challenges his new administration would face. His eyes narrowed and he spoke with focused intensity that revealed a relentless spirit. Whether I agreed with the prospect or not, I instantly sensed a second intervention in Iraq was in the making. I did not at that time, however, anticipate a US-led intervention in Afghanistan or a global war against terrorism.

Today, we have all three. The war against terrorism began as a stellar example of global cooperation, with the multinational intervention in Afghanistan as its centerpiece. The later intervention in Iraq, despite a façade of partnership, was mostly a US affair, with global divisiveness as its most prominent feature. The Afghanistan intervention properly sought to displace a regime that had given terrorists both sanctuary and support; indeed, it succeeded in toppling the Taliban and scattering Al Qaeda to the wind. The Iraq intervention, hastily based on thin information about weapons of mass destruction, ironically caused that nation – which already had long-standing ties to terrorists – to become a center in the war against terrorism as extremists flocked there to battle the United States. At present, the United States and its allies are engaged in state-building in both countries, with Afghanistan arguably having advanced the most. Still, the future of neither country appears secure.

Well in advance of the Iraq intervention, I warned that US involvement there would be costly, casualty-ridden and long in duration. I also criticized the Bush administration's timing of the intervention. But events overtook that debate long ago; the common interest now lies in confronting and stopping the terrorist threat in Iraq and in securing that nation's stability. With the insurgency raging and political progress slow, critics are advocating a timetable to withdraw American troops – the opposite of what is required, in my opinion.

Bush is right to urge Americans not to give up, but he must offer them a more compelling strategy than he has advanced to date. Instead of tempting them with the possibility of bringing some US troops home in 2006, the administration should consider innovative ways to boost the number of allied troops in the short term. That is necessary to secure the promise of December's elections in Iraq. A premature announcement of withdrawal plans would simply embolden the insurgents, including Saddam Hussein holdovers, Al Qaeda and other foreign terrorists.

It is worth emphasizing that foreign terrorists in Iraq present a major threat for the broader world. The Iraq intervention has given them a training opportunity unlike any they have seen since the Taliban period in Afghanistan. It would be unwise to underestimate their intentions or willingness to use Iraq as a staging area, should the Bush administration succumb to pressure to withdraw, with ensuing chaos. A similar, persistent, long-term effort is required in Afghanistan, where the Taliban and other extremists have resurfaced with a vengeance, in part because the state-building effort there has been less than robust.

The United States and the rest of the global community should take state-building in those countries and elsewhere in the world more seriously. After all, failed or failing states create environments for terrorism to breed. In the worst case scenarios, the governments in failed or failing states can become sponsors of terrorism. But even short of that, weak governments have limited means, which can leave terrorists a substantially free hand to organize, train, recruit and plot.

The situations in Iraq and Afghanistan are, of course, only two elements in the broad panorama of global terrorism challenges and threats. Four years ago, when the Bush administration launched the war against terrorism, the problem was suddenly in focus because of 9/11. However, the difficulty of waging a war with a non-traditional, largely invisible adversary which perpetually evolves has been abundantly evident.

Indeed, the very nature of the terrorist adversary places an obligation on the United States and its allies to think, strategize and act more creatively. That idea was the foundation for a conversation Sloan and I began more than a year ago, when he conceived the idea of calling a global gathering of top terrorism and counter-terrorism specialists to address the record of the war against terrorism, assess current and potential threats and produce policy recommendations. It was one of those "creation" moments, which Sloan understands well, given his own presence at the establishment of formal terrorism studies in the US academic world. He developed the first terrorism course in a US college or university curriculum at the University of Oklahoma.

To make a long story short, the discussion culminated in the University of Central Florida's hosting of an extraordinary conference the first week of November 2005. High-level specialists in various fields from dozens of countries traveled to Orlando for several days of intensive working sessions. Brian Jenkins, senior adviser to the president of RAND Corporation and a participant in the conference, summarized the challenge by indicating it is impossible to forecast, with any confidence, the future trajectory of terrorism. The problem will almost certainly persist, he said and it plainly has worsened. The possibility of terrorists' acquiring and using weapons of mass destruction may top the list of many people's concerns, but Jenkins advised that, with or without such devices, "terrorists will surprise us with attacks that could profoundly affect our society. We remain vulnerable. We are sliding into complacency. Whatever we do must be consistent with our values. This is no matter of mere morality. It is a strategic imperative. To ignore this is to risk alienation and isolation."

Other conference participants, facilitated by Sloan, rose to the challenge with some preliminary recommendations that will be developed into a white paper. I will not attempt to list all of those thoughts but will simply mention some of the more compelling ones. I especially liked the idea of a generation-long effort to bolster the public psyche and minimize the shock and surprise that terrorism can cause by providing widespread education about the phenomenon's sources, reach, intentions and future potential, as part of a broader push to spotlight global studies. I also believe, as the conference participants did, that it is essential to push governmental agencies here and in other countries toward the kind of cooperation that the terrorists practice. Further, I believe it is vital to shift the focus of the war against terrorism to the local level, where it originates. Terrorists may act globally and ignore national borders, but they have local roots and support systems, which argues for customized counter-terrorism strategies. Another worthwhile piece of advice stemming from the conference is that any strategy with an "America-first" component must be avoided.

Beyond that, we should pay more attention to specialists such as Sloan – and not the instant "experts" who materialized in droves after 9/11 – who have long worked to decipher the mysteries of terrorism. They do not seek attention and glory; rather, they endeavor to expand awareness and access to multiple perspectives, as Sloan does in this book – not only in his main text but also in the chronology and recommendations for further reading. It is worthwhile, incisive reading for those seeking to understand an imposing subject-area that is characterized by uncertainty, rapid change and extreme violence – and that will affect our lives for generations to come.

John C. Bersia
Special Assistant to the President
for Global Perspectives and
University Professor,
University of Central Florida,
Foreign Affairs Columnist,
Orlando Sentinel

Introduction

Imagery and Reality

With any luck, none of the readers of this book will ever experience the pain and anguish that is the result of an act of terrorism. This does not mean, however, that they and their families will not be affected by what they have witnessed through various forms of news media. But, this emotional and psychological impact will be second hand. As Brian Jenkins insightfully noted many years ago, 'terrorism is aimed at the people watching.'[1] Consequently, terrorism is a second-hand experience to most of us, an experience based on images that create a perception of a threat to our already often pressurized lives. Events such as 9/11 and other terrorist attacks force us to adjust to a violent reality, one which, because of television coverage, is not necessarily clear: the line between victim and spectator is often blurred. It is precisely the second-hand experience of the spectator that has made terrorism such a potent force. The actions of a small terrorist group are magnified through the lenses of the media to create an impact far beyond the number of individuals killed or injured.

Sun Tzu, the Asian sage on warfare, made a point that is synonymous with the impact of modern terrorism, "kill one person and frighten ten thousand."[2] With the events of 9/11 as well as the London and Madrid bombings, though, the numerical magnitude of terrorism has increased to "kill almost three thousand and frighten millions." Contemporary terrorists have modified the military technique of force multiplication to generate more physical and psychological bang for the buck. By their actions, the terrorists engage in what can be called "fear multiplication."

The object of this book is to counter the fear multiplication that has made terrorism such an effective weapon against the public and the international order. This will be by looking beyond the imagery of carnage that both attracts and repels the mass audience and by placing the threats and acts in an appropriate context that will not minimize the challenges we all face, but will help modify a primary emotional reaction or the attempt to tune out violence we indirectly witness on an almost daily basis.

This book is not intended solely to inform the reader. I hope that the reader, in his or her own right, will engage in a form of fear reduction to a more personal audience of family and friends. To this end I have included an Appendix that seeks to make it easier for the reader to take what he or she has learned and share it with others. The material within is also not meant solely for adults. Along with an adult audience, there was also a younger audience who witnessed the constant replays of aircraft crashing into the twin towers of the World Trade Center. Just as many adults were unable to process what they were seeing, so was this younger audience without the capacity to process what they saw. Many viewed the images even when their parents sought to shield them from it. The images were viewed everywhere. This, coupled with the ongoing targeting of civilians, *including* children, should be more than enough cause to prepare even those who are still deemed innocent.

This book can be used, I hope, as a basis for understanding a reality of life – no matter how disturbing it is – that should be addressed openly with all ages, especially those who are younger and often victims of overactive imaginations. I am not suggesting that all of the material within can or should be digested by a younger audience, but it can provide a foundation for discussion and understanding, and achieve a degree of fear reduction.

In addition to providing the context to understand terrorism by presenting and discussing its major characteristics, this book will also focus on presenting a brief history of its development. This historical approach will address the continuity and change that has characterized individuals, groups, acts and campaigns of terrorism and their tactics and strategies. It will also provide a basis to discern future trends of terrorism – a form of physical, psychological and political violence that has proven to be a type of protracted conflict and warfare not only enduring but growing, evolving and continuing to be a threat in the global environment.

To assist readers in understanding both the change and continuity in terrorism over the years, I have included a chronology listing specific events mentioned in the text, as well as some others worthy of note. Also, to the same end, I have included a list of further reading, some of it more detailed, for the reader who wishes to go further in his or her understanding. The volumes listed are only some of the many excellent books that look at terrorism and its result.

In combining the major characteristics and continuity and change which mark the evolution of terrorism, I will also identify and analyze each of the major characteristics and utilize a number of terrorist events – famous and unknown, conventional and unique – to illustrate them. From the analysis, the goal is to provide the basis for a necessary discussion of terrorism that can help family, friends and communities to cope better in what has aptly been called "an age of fear." This age is not only the result of the acts of terrorists, but by a public that has amplified the fear by focusing on the images instead of the nature, characteristics, dynamics and outcomes of terrorism.

Consequently, this book will also include a guide to enable groups – ranging from a family to a class to a civil club – to systematically address the nature of terrorism. It is hoped that in doing so, the words of President Roosevelt will resonate with the fact that we must learn how to live with terrorism, but more so, to live with the fear that it causes: "the only thing we have to fear is fear itself."

Chronology of Modern International Terrorism

This chronology is meant to assist the reader in understanding the continuity and change of terrorism over time and borrows heavily from the US Department of State's *Significant Terrorist Incidents, 1961–2003: A Brief Chronology* and the National Memorial Institute for the Prevention of Terror's Terrorism Knowledge Base (<http://www.tkb.org>). In no way is this chronology meant to be exhaustive, nor does it pretend to encompass all important events within modern international terrorism.

Some of the events list reasons for their significance and many do not, since while some events were included in the list for their import, many were included to give the reader a well-rounded picture of the many forms terrorism can take.

Assassins

The assassins were a Muslim sect active during the eighth to fourteenth centuries. Their formal name was *al-daʿwa al-jadīda* but because they were accused of chewing hashish, they were called *hashishin*. Individual assassins would receive an order to kill someone – usually a political figure – and would carry out the attacks, often in broad daylight. The assassins' weapon of choice was a dagger, nearly always fatal at a close range when used by someone skilled, but this advantage virtually guaranteed the attacker's capture or killing.

Zealots

The Zealots were a Jewish sect in the first century CE bent on evicting Roman power from Israel. The one extreme group of Zealots was also known in Latin as *sicarii*, "daggermen" (sing. *sicarius*), because of their policy of assassinating Jews opposed to their call for war against Rome. The Zealots played a lead role in the Jewish Revolt in the middle of the first century.

1789–1799: French Revolution, the Reign of Terror

The "Reign of Terror" was a period during the French Revolution characterized by mass oppression and mass executions. It was ostensibly to eliminate enemies within the new democratic French state, though much more likely it was to eliminate opposition to the new government. During its time of greatest activity, estimated numbers of its victims vary from 18,000 to 40,000 killed. The Reign of Terror is an example of state terrorism that carries over to current time. Executions were public, to establish fear in those who might oppose the regime. State terrorism is used within countries to this day to intimidate the public into abandoning any opposition to the government.

July 22, 1968

On this date was the hijacking by the Popular Front for the Liberation of Palestine (PFLP) of an El Al flight from Rome to Tel Aviv by three armed terrorists from the PFLP, one of the subgroups of the Palestine Liberation Organization (PLO). The flight was diverted to Algiers where twenty-one passengers and eleven crew members remained captive for thirty-nine days.

This attack is thought by many to mark the internationalization of terrorism. While certainly not the first hijacking of a commercial airline, this hijacking made a statement both to the country being threatened – in this case Israel – and the rest of the world. It was the first hijacking where the airplane itself was used as a symbol and showed how willing terrorists were to go out of their own area to commit acts of terror. It created a situation where the country of Israel was forced to talk to the terrorists and their organization by the placing of a real threat of catastrophic destruction in the hands of those negotiating for hostage release.

July 21, 1972: Bloody Friday

An Irish Republican Army (IRA) bomb attack killed eleven people and injured 130 in Belfast, Northern Ireland. At least twenty bombs detonated across the city over the course of seventy-five minutes, not allowing any resident to feel safe. Ten days later, three IRA car bombs in the village of Claudy left six dead.

This was a culmination of the breakdown of talks between the IRA and the British government. Partly because of its sheer scale, it proved one of the most effective attacks in the history of terrorism.

September 5, 1972: Munich Massacre

Eight Palestinian "Black September" terrorists seized eleven Israeli athletes in the Olympic Village in Munich, West Germany. In a bungled rescue attempt by West German authorities, nine of the hostages (two others had already been killed) and five terrorists were killed.

Again, this is an incredible example of how terrorist organizations utilize the world media to get their message across. The Munich Massacre stands as one of the best-covered terrorist attacks, even given the mass media attention of September 11 and the Madrid and London bombings.

March 16, 1978: Kidnap and Assassination of Aldo Moro

In the prominent terrorist kidnapping of a high-level official, Italian Prime Minister Aldo Moro was seized by the Red Brigade and assassinated fifty-five days later. This is an example of a tactic still widely used.

November 4, 1979: Iran Hostage Crisis

After President Carter agreed to admit the Shah of Iran into the US, Iranian radicals seized the US Embassy in Tehran and took sixty-six American diplomats hostage. Of these, thirteen were soon released, but the remaining fifty-three were held until their release on January 20, 1981.

This is a primary example of how a nation-state might use a terrorist group as a front for plausible deniability. The "students" who took over the Embassy in Tehran were supported by the government, though the Iranians denied this.

This event brought nearly 24-hour-a-day coverage of the terrorists' cause, putting the media center stage in terms of terrorism. The news program *Nightline* was spawned from this media event and had the effect of making reporters themselves part of the media hype.

October 6, 1981: Assassination of Egyptian President Anwar Sadat

Soldiers, who were secret members of the *Takfir Wal-Hajira* sect, attacked and killed Egyptian President Anwar Sadat during a troop review and parade. The soldiers jumped out of a vehicle and, with grenades and gunfire, attacked the stands where Sadat was sitting. The assassination was only possible because of the group's infiltration of the military. Its significance stems both from this infiltration as well as the high level of the individual targeted.

October 31, 1984: Assassination of Indian Prime Minister Indira Gandhi

Premier Indira Gandhi was shot to death by members of her security force. Again we see the infiltration into positions close (in proximity) to a high-level official. This is also similar to the Sadat assassination in that the target was the leader of the country.

October 23, 1983: Bombing of Marine Barracks in Beirut

Near-simultaneous suicide truck-bomb attacks were made on US and French compounds in Beirut, Lebanon. A 12,000-pound bomb destroyed the US compound, killing 242 Americans, while fifty-eight French troops were killed when a 400-pound device destroyed a French base.

Islamic Jihad claimed responsibility. While the effectiveness in terms of destruction of lives is significant in this event, its most important attribute is that it demonstrates how effective a terrorist event can be. Many credit the Beirut Bombings with driving the US military out of the conflict in Lebanon.

October 12, 1984: Bombing of Conservative Party Conference, Brighton

The IRA placed a 100-pound bomb at the Brighton Grand Hotel to explode during the UK's Conservative Party Conference. Five people were killed and thirty-four injured in the blast, with Prime Minister Margaret Thatcher and members of her Cabinet narrowly escaping death in the explosion.

Patrick Magee was eventually charged and convicted of the bombings. Magee had allegedly been trained at a terrorist training center in Libya, showing collaboration between terrorist organizations with seemingly little in common.

May 21, 1991: Assassination of Former Indian Prime Minister Rajiv Gandhi

A female member of the Liberation Tigers of Tamil Elam (LTTE) killed herself, Prime Minister Rajiv Gandhi and sixteen others by detonating an explosive vest after presenting a garland of flowers to him during an election rally in the Indian state of Tamil Nadu. This attack demonstrates that female terrorists and suicide bombers are not new phenomena.

February 26, 1993: World Trade Center Bombing

The World Trade Center in New York City was badly damaged when a car bomb planted by Islamic terrorists exploded in an underground garage. The bomb left six people dead and 1,000 injured. The men carrying out the attack were followers of Umar Abd al-Rahman, an Egyptian cleric who preached in the New York City area. This was the first major attack on US soil by Islamist terrorists. Many view it as a precursor to the September 11 attacks.

February 25, 1994: Hebron Massacre

Jewish right-wing extremist and US citizen Baruch Goldstein machine-gunned Moslem worshippers at a mosque in the West Bank town of Hebron, killing twenty-nine and wounding about 150. While the Palestinian–Israeli conflict continues, it is good to remember that terrorism has existed on both sides.

April 19, 1995: Bombing of Oklahoma City Federal Building

Right-wing extremists Timothy McVeigh and Terry Nichols destroyed the Federal Building in Oklahoma City with a massive truck bomb that killed 166 and injured hundreds more in what was, up to then, the largest terrorist attack on American soil.

January 31, 1996: Tamil Tigers Attack

Members of LTTE rammed an explosives-laden truck into the Central Bank in the heart of downtown Colombo, Sri Lanka, killing ninety civilians and injuring more than 1,400 others, including two US citizens.

February 26, 1996: Hamas Bus Attack

In Jerusalem, a suicide bomber blew up a bus, killing twenty-six, including three US citizens and injuring some eighty others. This is an attack that exemplifies a tactic Hamas long used in Israel that was eventually adopted by one of the attackers in London in 2005.

May 1978–April 1996: Unabomber

Over the span of eighteen years Theodore Kaczynski, better known as the Unabomber, conducted a campaign of terror against personal enemies and people he viewed as contributing to the increasing dominance of technology. Kaczynski's brother eventually turned him in to the police.

The significance of the Unabomber is that he demonstrated the ability of a single individual with no organizational affiliations to cause widespread panic and terror.

December 3, 1996: Paris Subway Explosion

A bomb exploded aboard a Paris Metro (subway) train as it arrived at the Port Royal station, killing two French nationals, a Moroccan and a Canadian and injuring eighty-six others. Among those injured were one US citizen and another Canadian. No one claimed responsibility for the attack, but Algerian extremists were suspected.

August 7, 1998: US Embassy Bombings in East Africa

A bomb exploded at the rear entrance of the US Embassy in Nairobi, Kenya, killing twelve US citizens, thirty-two Foreign Service Nationals (FSNs) and 247 Kenyan citizens. Approximately 5,000 Kenyans, six US citizens and thirteen FSNs were injured. The US Embassy building sustained extensive structural damage.

Almost simultaneously, a bomb detonated outside the US Embassy in Dar es Salaam, Tanzania, killing seven FSNs and three Tanzanian citizens and injuring one US citizen and seventy-six Tanzanians. The explosion caused major structural damage to the US Embassy facility and the US Government held Osama Bin Laden responsible.

August 15, 1998: IRA Bombing, Omagh

A 500-pound car bomb planted by the Real IRA exploded outside a local courthouse in the central shopping district of Omagh, Northern Ireland, killing twenty-nine people and injuring more than 330 others.

October 12, 2000: Attack on USS Cole

In Aden, Yemen, a small dinghy carrying explosives rammed the destroyer USS *Cole*, killing seventeen sailors and injuring thirty-nine others. Supporters of Osama Bin Laden were suspected.

September 9, 2001: Death of "the Lion of the Panjshir"

Two suicide bombers fatally wounded Ahmed Shah Massoud, a leader of Afghanistan's Northern Alliance, which had opposed both the Soviet occupation and the post-Soviet Taliban government. The bombers posed as journalists and were apparently linked to Al Qaeda. The Northern Alliance did not confirm Massoud's death until September 15.

September 11, 2001: Terrorist Attacks on US Homeland

Two hijacked airliners crashed into the twin towers of the World Trade Center. Soon thereafter, a third hijacked plane struck the Pentagon. A fourth hijacked plane, suspected to be bound for a high-profile target in Washington, crashed into a field in southern

Pennsylvania. The attacks killed 3,025 US citizens and other nationals. President Bush and Cabinet officials indicated that Osama Bin Laden was the prime suspect and that they considered the United States in a state of war with international terrorism. In the aftermath of the attacks, the United States brought together the Global Coalition Against Terrorism.

Widely considered the formative attack in modern international terrorism, September 11 "changed the form of terrorism." It marked for many a new and more deadly type of terror where mass casualties were the goal. Unlike attacks from Aum Shinrikyo that used a potential Weapon of Mass Destruction (see chapter 4), the September 11 terrorists used a relatively conventional method of attack to inflict the single greatest terrorist event the world had ever seen.

October/November 2001: Anthrax Attacks

On October 7 the US Centers for Disease Control and Prevention (CDC) reported that investigators had detected evidence that the deadly anthrax bacterium was present in the building where a Florida man who died of anthrax on October 5 had worked. Discovery of a second anthrax case triggered a major investigation by the Federal Bureau of Investigation (FBI).

The two anthrax cases were the first to appear in the United States in twenty-five years. Anthrax subsequently appeared in mail received by television networks in New York and by the offices in Washington of Senate Majority Leader Tom Daschle and other members of Congress. Attorney General John Ashcroft said in a briefing on October 16, "When people send anthrax through the mail to hurt people and invoke terror, it's a terrorist act." This is one of only a handful of examples of terrorist organizations or individuals successfully using a biological weapon.

January 23, 2002: Kidnapping of Daniel Pearl

Armed militants kidnapped *Wall Street Journal* reporter Daniel Pearl in Karachi, Pakistan. Pakistani authorities received videotape on February 20 depicting Pearl's murder. His grave was found near Karachi on May 16. Pakistani authorities arrested four suspects, of whom Ringleader Ahmad Omar Saeed Sheikh claimed to have organized Pearl's kidnapping to protest Pakistan's subservience to the United States and had belonged to Jaish-e-Muhammad, an Islamic separatist group in Kashmir. All four suspects were convicted on July 15. Saeed Sheikh was sentenced to death, the others to life imprisonment.

The Daniel Pearl kidnapping captured America's attention because of his US citizenship as well as his normally protected status as a journalist. The video of Pearl's murder is also a prime example of how terrorist groups are using the internet to reach a larger audience.

October 12, 2002: Car Bomb Explosion in Bali

A car bomb exploded outside the Sari Club Discotheque in Denpasar, Bali, Indonesia, killing 202 persons and wounding 300 more. Most of the casualties, including eighty-eight of the dead, were Australian tourists. Seven US citizens were among the dead. Al Qaeda claimed responsibility and two suspects were later arrested and convicted, with Iman Samudra, who had trained in Afghanistan with Al Qaeda and was suspected of belonging to Jemaah Islamiya, sentenced to death. He was executed by firing squad on September 10, 2003.

October 23–26, 2002: Chechen Rebels Seize a Moscow Theater

Fifty Chechen rebels led by Movsar Barayev seized the Palace of Culture Theater in Moscow, Russia, to demand an end to the war in Chechnya. They seized more than 800 hostages from thirteen countries and threatened to blow up the theater. During a three-day siege, they killed a Russian policeman and five Russian hostages.

On October 26, Russian Special Forces pumped an anesthetic gas through the ventilation system and then stormed the theater. All of the rebels were killed, but ninety-four hostages (including one American) also died, many from the effects of the gas. A group led by Chechen warlord Shamil Basayev claimed responsibility. This attack shows that Islamist terror not only is a threat to Western Europe and the United States, but is used throughout the world.

March 28, 2003

In Rome, extremists firebombed a dealership for Ford and Jaguar, two brands of automobile taken as symbols of the Anglo-American coalition that is fighting in Iraq. Approximately a dozen Fords were burned and another ten damaged. A five-pointed star, a symbol of the Red Brigade, was found at the site; however, the Red Brigade is not known to plan firebomb attacks and no one claimed responsibility. This attack shows the ability of terrorist organizations to become mantles for others to adopt, whether or not the actual attackers were affiliated with the group.

May 19, 2003

At about 6:00 a.m. in French Hill Intersection, Northern Jerusalem, a suicide bomber dressed as an Orthodox Jew and wearing a prayer shawl boarded a commuter bus and detonated the bombs he had attached to himself. Victims included seven killed and twenty-six wounded (including one US citizen), according to press reports. The Islamic Resistance Movement (Hamas) claimed responsibility for this attack.

August 19, 2003: Bombing of the UN Headquarters in Baghdad

A truck loaded with surplus Iraqi ordnance exploded outside the United Nations Headquarters in Baghdad's Canal Hotel. A hospital across the street was also heavily damaged. The twenty-three dead included UN Special Representative Sergio Viera de Mello. More than 100 persons were wounded. It was not clear whether the bomber was a Baath Party loyalist or a foreign Islamic militant. An Al Qaeda branch called the Brigades of the Martyr Abu Hafz al-Masri later claimed responsibility.

March 11, 2004: Madrid Bombings

During the morning, in Madrid, 10 bombs exploded on the city's commuter transit system, killing 191 people and wounding approximately 1,900. The bombs, hidden in backpacks, were placed in stations and on trains along a single rail line. By the end of March, Spanish authorities had arrested more than twenty people in connection with the attacks. On April 3, 2004, a key figure in the attacks blew himself up, along with six other suspects, in his apartment after police surrounded the building.

The Abu Hafts al-Mari Brigades, on behalf of Al Qaeda and several other groups claimed responsibility, but Spanish authorities are investigating an Al Qaeda-affiliated network with transnational ties to Pakistan, Spain, Morocco, Algeria, Tunisia and Syria and possible links to the September 11, 2001 attacks in the United States. This large-scale attack exemplifies why "modern terrorists" are difficult to capture. Not only are they willing to die for their causes, but their international ties are difficult to track.

March 22, 2004

Sheikh Ahmad Yassin was killed by an Israeli missile while he was traveling in a car. Yassin was the religious leader of Hamas, the Islamic Resistance Movement based in Palestine. Israel has continued to assassinate those who it feels are the perpetrators of terror within its boundaries.

September 1, 2004: Beslan School Incident

At 10:20 a.m., in North Ossetia, Beslan, Russia, thirty-two armed men and women seized School Number 1 on the first day of the new school year, taking more than 1,300 people hostage for two days, allowing them little or no food or water. On September 3, 2004, an explosion inside the gymnasium where hostages were held sparked a fierce gun battle between the hostage-takers and security forces.

According to official figures, 331 people were killed, 172 of them children, though many believe the actual number of deaths was higher. More than 600 others were injured. The Riyadh us-Saliheyn Martyrs' Brigade claimed responsibility.

March 24, 2005

A suicide bomber set off his truck bomb at a checkpoint in Ramadi in Iraq, killing eleven Iraqi Special Forces Police and wounding at least fourteen others. The Islamic Army in Iraq claimed responsibility for the attack, which is exemplary of many suicide attacks now occurring in Iraq.

July 7, 2005: London 1

Four suicide bombers struck in central London, killing fifty-two people and injuring 700. The coordinated attacks hit the transport system as the morning rush hour drew to a close. Three bombs went off at 8:50 a.m. BST on London Underground (subway) trains just outside stations on Liverpool Street and Edgeware Road and on another train while traveling. The final explosion was around an hour later on a double-decker bus.

Four suicide bombers were later identified as the perpetrators of the attack. All were British citizens. These attacks highlighted the problems with growing extremism within countries not only in the Islamic world, but worldwide.

July 21, 2005: London 2

Four attempted bombings took place in London exactly two weeks after the July 7 attacks. It was the same type of operation. Four failed bombs were found, three on London Underground trains and one on a bus. Four suspects were arrested and charged with the attempted bombings.

October 1, 2005

In Bali, three bombs ripped through as many restaurants killing twenty-five people. This was an attack on the anniversary of the Bali bombings in 2002. Suicide bombers were determined to mirror the method of the earlier bombings, this considered devastating for Bali's tourist industry.

–1–

The Meaning of Terrorism
Cutting through the Semantic Jungle

In the academic, political and operational world of terrorism, there is little agreement on the definition of terrorism. Existing definitions range from "you know it when you see it" to the most complex formulations that appear to have been jerry-built – and indeed, a number of them have been by committee. In fact, according to one leading authority, there are more than two hundred recognized definitions and even each one of them can be subject to interpretation.[1]

It is not that the definitional issue is not important. At the outset, the definition can help to establish what the scope of the inquiry is. That is, how does one differentiate acts of terrorism from other forms of violence? Moreover, the question of definition has both policy and operational implications. For example, if terrorism is primarily considered to be a criminal act, the focus is on law enforcement – a primarily preventative and reactive approach with a minimum use of force and strong emphasis on the collection of evidence. If, on the other hand, terrorism is viewed to be a form of warfare, the focus would be a military approach with an emphasis on collection of intelligence for planning operations – an offensive approach and, as required, a maximum use of force.

Perhaps the most vexing of all of this is that the word "terrorism" is itself an emotionally laden one. As the saying goes: one man's terrorist is another man's freedom fighter. In sum, terrorism is largely defined on the basis of one's ideological and political vantage point. This is to be expected, since the use of terrorism in both rhetoric and action has taken on a pejorative meaning. Therefore, while it may be intellectually stimulating to debate its meaning, debates on definition often lead to frustration and semantic deadlock.

It may be more useful to parse the definition of terrorism by identifying its major characteristics. By effectively dissecting the anatomy of terrorism, one can have a basis for understanding its major characteristics without falling into the emotional and political motivation that often accompanies the definition issue. What are the major characteristics of terrorism? An enunciation of discussion of each not only provides the framework for the following chapters, but also places terrorism in a context that goes beyond imagery and emotional reaction.

Terrorism is not Mindless Violence: It's an Instrumental Act

The image of a suicide bomber in Sri Lanka, Israel or Iraq; the killing of children in Russia; the poisoning of passengers in a subway in Tokyo and other acts of carnage reinforce the view that terrorists are deranged individuals whose motivation for action is either unfathomable, primal or both. While on occasion an individual may be mentally ill, most are quite rational in their actions. It is because the public can neither understand nor justify what they have witnessed that the perpetrators are characterized as being sociopaths or, in a more colloquial sense, crazies. That public perception is largely predicated on the view that what the terrorists do is not rational. Somehow, ascribing rationality to an action is viewed as justifying it. The tragic fact is that one moves toward the dehumanization process used to describe adversaries in war. We are therefore forced to recognize the "ordinariness" of most terrorists. They represent what Hannah Arendt referred to in regard to Adolf Eichman, the organizer of mass killings and genocide, who was a manifestation of "the banality of evil."[2]

When individuals resort to acts of violence as individuals or members of a particular group – no matter how repugnant – they are involved in a form of collective behavior as part of a larger ideology. In the fullest sense, terrorism is purposeful violence.

To achieve some goal – short- or long-term, realistic or fantastical – it should be recognized that terrorism, in most cases, is instrumental – a means to an end and a way to achieve various goals. An understanding of the purposeful act provides the necessary basis to understand terrorism. The understanding brings necessary analytic order and a degree of objectivity that would be impossible to achieve if one simply said that terrorism was just mindless violence. This understanding does not suggest that there are not those who for whatever reason engage in violence for violence's sake, but most individuals and groups involved in terrorism are goal-directed – not only in regard to objectives achieved in this life but, as in the case of suicide bombers, also the next.

Terrorism as Strategy and Tactics

Since those who engage in terrorism are not involved in mindless violence, what brings a sense of direction, planning and cohesion to the individual acts and campaigns of terrorism? Similar to the case of its definition, the line between strategies and tactics may be blurred.

Strategy refers to the big picture – the broader and ultimate goals of an organization, be it military or civilian. In contrast, *tactics* refer to those measures that are utilized to achieve strategic objectives. In understanding the characteristics of terrorism, the arbitrary division between the two is often obscured.

To many terrorist groups, particularly those motivated by fundamentalist religious beliefs, the strategy is both preordained and transcendental. The ultimate objective will become a reality based on one's religious belief or a commitment to a particular ideology. It is set in stone by either religious interpretation or a worldview based on a particular vision of human nature and history. In some ways strategy is faith in a certain outcome, rather than an objective that will be ultimately realized, by the "true believer."[3] This interpretation of strategy is akin to dogma – it is the revealed truth that, while subject to some interpretation, is immutable.

Consequently, the strategy often addresses very broad goals which can be defined in terms of religious transformations or the secular assertion of a political ideology. Even here the line is blurred because to the religious fundamentalist the line between Church and State, the divine and the secular, does not exist. Thus, the individuals and groups who adhere to fundamental beliefs need not be concerned with addressing tactics because all will be accomplished as articles of faith – that is, the terrorist knows that his or her success is ordained and, therefore, cannot fail. Whether an anarchist group that seeks to destroy the old order or a religious group that seeks to replace another, there is no need to define the tactics in a world where the present and future have already been ordained. The vision may be faulty and cannot objectively be achieved, but that makes no difference. Despite the hardships and barriers in the communities of both the religious and the secular, the strategy will be realized as an article of faith.

This does not mean that religious and secular tactics don't have a part to play in the pursuit of the ultimate goal, but such tactics are short-term, part of a temporal world, fleeting and may or may not be connected to the strategic vision. It is this blurring of the line between tactics and strategy that is both a great strength and a great weakness to those who engage in terrorism.

The strength of having a strategic vision rests in the fact that, whatever the odds or setbacks, those who believe in the vision can engage in a protracted conflict against great adversaries with the firm realization not only that their cause is just, but that, given time, its goals will be achieved. In contrast, governments opposing terrorism – particularly democracies – must address the continuing shift of public opinion, contentious and fractious political forces, competition for tangible resources and diverse policy alternatives. And all of this must be done to address effectively any immediate and short-term crises. Despite the desire to have a strategic vision, governments have little time to address long-term strategic goals. Forced to address what may be considered tactical considerations, the political leadership does not have the luxury to think, much less act, strategically against adversaries with a long-term commitment.

The pressure to do something in the face of the latest terrorist act places intense pressure on governments. Even the attempt to focus on the tactical dimensions of combating terrorism is fraught with difficulties. Since most terrorist groups do not differentiate between civilians, the military and law-enforcement personnel, they all exist as a global target of opportunity. The public demands effective security measures as if total protection could be provided. This is an impossibility because the results would be an undemocratic transformation of the political order, replaced with a repressive "surveillance society."[4] How does one establish the appropriate cost for security in monetary, liberty and political currencies? This does not suggest that there are not tactical measures that can effectively counter threats and acts of terrorism, but they are beyond the scope of this book.

What is most important, strategically and tactically, is what the reader and his or her family, friends and community can do to meet the threat. The basic requirement of doing so is to understand terrorism and to respond neither blindly nor emotionally to the images which bombard us on a daily basis. In order to develop the necessary understanding, one must address the following question: What are the various forms of terrorism and how do they impact the immediate victims and the audience?

Terrorism as a Form of Individual and Collective Psychological Operations

Since terrorism is violence with a purpose, what is its prime goal? On this there appears to be a consensus by most authorities despite problems associated with seeking a universal definition. Terrorism is first and foremost a form of psychological warfare. As noted earlier, the attacks are primarily instigated to affect the audience. This does suggest that the death, pain and anguish of the immediate victims is not very real and important, but it is the second-order effect – the impact on a broader audience – that makes terrorism such an invidious and profound weapon. If you recognize the psychological objectives of the terrorist toward individuals and groups, there is a better chance that you can better adjust to the realities of terrorism. This lessens the magnification of the threat that causes one to engage in what can rightfully be called auto-terrorism – that is, the terrorizing of oneself.

The impact of terrorism on the individual is intimately related to the nature of terror. As a pioneering report noted, "terror is a natural phenomenon; terrorism is the conscious exploitation of it."[5] Terror is a mental state, primarily a fear of what might happen to us. All of us have varying degrees of stated and unstated concerns about situations that create a sense of fear or dread within. In most instances they lie below the mental surface and do not have an impact on our behavior, but when a fear is so strong that it rises to our consciousness and has a profound impact on our mental well being and physical behavior, it can become a phobia. Phobias can paralyze both individuals and societies, which is why it is vital that we do not react primally when we hear of a terrorist attack.

We all have various agendas of fear, things that can intimidate us, things that go bump in the night. In most instances we grow out of them. But, terrorists have created an agenda of fear that can influence our behavior. For example, while the public may have some generalized concerns about flying, most individuals will fly since it is the fastest and most convenient form of long-distance travel. While passenger traffic increased because of availability and price, since the introduction of skyjacking in the 1960s most people will look around their gate at the airport and profile other passengers, asking themselves how they would react if their concerns become a reality. They have become secondary victims of terrorism. When their behavior changes and they won't fly because of terrorist acts, they become first-hand victims of terrorism. While they are not the immediate victims held hostage in a cabin, they have fallen victim because it has changed both their mental and physical behaviors.

Governments which practice terrorism from above – regime repression – have also created agendas of fear to change attitudes and behaviors and enforce compliance among their citizens. The classic technique of arresting individuals at night, the shock of being taken away from the warmth and security of a bed by the police, has tempered individuals who would normally speak out against a government and its policies. Even more invidious is the fact that a government, through psychological manipulation, will seek to probe the weaknesses and fears of someone and use the threat of turning those fears into a reality as a means of seeking confession or enforcing compliance. One need only remember how the protagonist in George Orwell's *1984* was broken by the government who recognized his fear of being eaten by rats.[6]

When people identify with a victim of terrorism whom they have seen on television or read about, when they can not only relate to the experience but also think "there but for the grace of God go I," then they have been subject to terrorism. If the terrorist's actions have altered the way someone both thinks and behaves, then the audience member has been subject to a degree of terrorism that can be measured from mild to profound. The impact on the individual who witnesses, but is not directly involved in, an incident of terrorism cannot be overstated. The ability to reach out electronically and touch someone in so many ways has given terrorists the ability to export fear consciously beyond the immediate victim. How to counter that fear will be discussed in the Appendix.

The magnitudes of acts of terrorism have been greatly enhanced by the fact that not only are individuals subject to fear and terrorism, but also that society at large is subject to the impact of terrorist acts and campaigns. If terrorism is ultimately aimed at creating a psychological effect on the individual, then it is also a form of psychological warfare geared at mass audiences and the governments that represent them. The success of terrorism is not only in the magnification of its acts through threat and its physical coercion of the immediate victim, but also in the psycho-social coercion against a much larger group.

Terrorism is very successful as a fear multiplier. This multiplication is primarily the result of acts of terrorism breaking through our individual and collective desire for predictability and the accompanying sense of security. Beyond the earthly considerations is also the more transcendental impact. In the final analysis, the violence the public witnesses reminds them not only of their own vulnerability, but also of their own mortality.

This sense of vulnerability and mortality is readily seen among members of communities that have been subject to terrorists' attacks both directly and indirectly. Directly, as in the case of the Oklahoma City bombing or the World Trade Center attacks, where numerous people could literally say that if they had not been late to work or chosen to take the day off, they could have been in the ruins of the destroyed buildings. One can only imagine the long-term psychological impact on those individuals, but even more disturbing is the indirect psychological impact on the part of those who could have been victims. Those who witnessed the carnage from five or five thousand miles away share a common emotion in an interconnected world. Their sense of security has been threatened and, ironically, those closer to the act may be better able to cope than those further away.

Consider the following: Students who are in Spain during a bombing in Madrid may have the luxury of telling their parents not to worry since they were miles away on the coast. But, to the parents, distance may be irrelevant because in their eyes their children were in Spain when the attack happened. Perhaps the most coherent illustration that distance may not determine the magnitude of the psychological impact is the unfortunate trend in the seizure of schoolchildren. Attacks may be politically motivated as what happened in South Malacca, in the Netherlands and in Beslan, Russia or non-political such as the murders of high school students by fellow students in Columbine, Colorado. Such tragedies create intense psychological pain. The children were deliberately selected as targets because their captivity, injury or death strikes at the very heart of the family structure. By their actions, the perpetrators send a chilling message to the world. Now, after 9/11, the United States understands that terrorism is not what happens to someone else in some other country.

Terrorism as a Political Weapon

If a psychological impact is central to the tactics and strategies of those who practice terrorism, then it is equally true that in terms of goals the primary focus of terrorism is to achieve political objectives, as Bruce Hoffman states in his text *Inside Terrorism,* "terrorism is ineluctably political."[7] Terrorists have mixed agendas, ranging from organized crime to religious crusades, but there is a common agreement that what differentiates terrorism from other forms of violence is its political dimension. Thus, while someone may be taken hostage during a bank robbery and subjected to terror, they are not victims of terrorism. To the victim, the motivation behind the action might not be significant, but to the authorities it can make quite a bit of difference. Different measures are taken when combating terrorism as opposed to apolitical criminal acts.

Terrorism is first and foremost a weapon used to promote a political agenda. It should be emphasized that terrorists come from all sides of the political spectrum. They range from those who wish to destroy the system to those who want to revolutionize the system and those who wish to return to an idealized system of the past. Those who have had the greatest capability in performing acts of mass terrorism hold yet another position on the political spectrum, those engaging in terrorism from above – the authoritarian and totalitarian states. Many examples of this type of terrorism exist in modern times, from the brutal crackdown on students in Burma in 1988 to the recent intimidation of the people of Zimbabwe by their President, Robert Mugabe.

It is also important to recognize that the position of politics in terrorism is not always clear. For example, some fundamentalist beliefs do not differentiate between religious and secular and thus no line differentiating Church and State exists. The lack of this differentiation has created one of the most potent forms of terrorism, Holy Terror, where an article of faith supersedes political ideology.[8]

The scope of political change desired may also vary from issue-oriented terrorism, such as the debate over the right to have abortions and specific environmental demands. In the broader range, the political objectives may be based on calls for self-determination based on ethnic, language and territorial considerations. Beyond that, as in the case of various fundamentalist groups, objectives go beyond the nation-state and seek regional or global changes through terrorism.

Given the diversity of belief systems by terrorists and their organizations, it is just as dangerous to engage in generalized terrorist stereotyping as it is to engage in simplistic physical, racial and ethnic stereotyping. Both types may bring superficial analytical order that provides simplistic and erroneous descriptions of who the terrorists are at the cost of being ineffective or even worse, promoting racism and other forms of prejudice and discrimination.

Terrorism as a Form of Warfare

It is common for the political leadership and the media to discuss policies in the context of the war on terrorism, but by no means is it clear whether it *is* a war and if so, what *kind* of war it is. As in the case of a general definition of terrorism, a discussion of terrorism as warfare is not simply semantic. There are policy and operational implications that result from this discussion.

At the outset, one must raise the issue of where terrorism fits into what is commonly referred to as the spectrum of conflict, which ranges from low intensity to mid-intensity to conventional to ultimately nuclear conflict. Traditionally, terrorism has been associated with unconventional or low-intensity conflict, which also fall under the heading of insurgency. In this context, terrorism is primarily viewed as an unconventional tactic in a territorial conflict waged by a weak organization against a strong adversary – most commonly the government in power. The insurgents (the weak side) engage in asymmetric warfare in which they attempt to overcome the strength of their enemy by playing on its vulnerabilities – a large number of targets, a cumbersome bureaucracy and often a low level of public acceptance of the conflict (i.e. legitimacy).[9]

Those who engage in this type of terrorism seek to wear down their adversary psychologically through a protracted campaign of conflict. This is often a tactic used as part of a revolutionary strategy. In this type of conflict, the small numbers and clandestine nature of the insurgents makes them difficult to identify, attack and apprehend. These types of terrorist campaigns are sometimes referred to as 'the war of the flea,' so aptly named in honor of the exceedingly small insect that is very difficult to eradicate.[10]

When terrorism is viewed as a form of unconventional territorially based insurgency, governments utilize two broad types of counter-insurgency program. One is called the systems approach – or internal defense development – where the object is to strengthen the police, the military and general coercive capabilities of the threatened government. The other way is the "hearts and minds" approach, which seeks to lessen or eliminate the terrorists' base of support by engaging in programs to win over the population. This approach relates to the Maoist doctrine that guerrillas are the fish who swim in the ocean of the people. By reducing the size of the ocean of popular support, the government has a greater opportunity to prevail.

With the advancing technologies in transportation and communication systems starting in the 1960s, we have witnessed the development of what I call "non-territorial terrorism" – a form of terrorism not confined to a clearly delineated geographic area.[11] As a result of the introduction of jet aircraft, terrorists could literally strike at targets of opportunity thousands of miles from the territorial-based conflict. Moreover, as the events of 9/11 showed us, non-territorial terrorists can use aircraft as what can be called a low-intensity human-guided intercontinental missile system. The balance of nuclear terror during the Cold War has now been upended by terrorists who have engaged in mass terror using planes as non-nuclear, but very potent, weapons of mass destruction.

Given the emergence of non-territorial terrorism, the counter-terrorism strategies and tactics that have applied to terrorism as part of an insurgency may no longer be appropriate. Since the terrorists have often selected targets far away from their base of operations, whose hearts and minds can a government win over? The victims of the attacks live nowhere near the terrorists' base. In conjunction with this, a third-party government may not only provide safe haven to the terrorists and their base of operations, but may also engage in supporting the terrorists who carry out operations beyond their borders, as was the case with Al Qaeda. When these attacks occur thousands of miles from where the terrorists make their home, a major challenge for the targeted government is the jurisdiction and territorial boundaries of its police, military and security forces.

Terrorism as a form of warfare has yet to be clearly defined by those who are schooled in the arts and sciences of warfare. This is not a traditional conflict between nation-states; nor is it a war with uniformed, recognizable soldiers. There are also no clearly defined laws of warfare or rules of engagement, since to all intents and purposes terrorism is a war that does not recognize the difference between combatant and noncombatant. If we do define it as war, it is a war without rules, a war without structure. In a sense, it is a new form of total war, though usually on a smaller scale.

By saying that terrorists do not recognize the difference between combatant and noncombatant I do not mean to suggest that civilians have not been killed or wounded as a result of war – often called collateral damage. The difference here is that terrorists intentionally target civilians as a prime objective in waging their psychological warfare.

Another manifestation caused by contemporary terrorism has resulted in a response by multinational corporations. Just as terrorists have created their own non-state armies, multinational corporations have developed their own counterterrorist forces. Governments have enlisted the aid of nongovernmental civilians on the battlefield to provide services for counterterrorist military operations. The new mercenary, the corporate warrior, has arisen.[12]

Finally, we are entering a new phase in the transformation of warfare with the emergence of netwar. Terrorists who reject secular Western culture, but are more than willing and capable to use the latest trends in technology against industrial and postindustrial societies, have been using it effectively. Netwar will be discussed further in chapter 6, with a greater look into the future of terrorism.

Terrorism as a Crime

As in the case of defining terrorism, there is a wide variety of different legal descriptions and degrees for what constitutes activities associated with terrorism. These activities range from sympathizing to providing support to planning the event to executing the act of terrorism. The effort of establishing an agreed upon corpus of law on the subject is further complicated by the utilization of different legal systems at the local, state, national and international levels. Nevertheless, in a broad sense there is recognition that terrorism, even if politically motivated, is a crime. The problem, however, is that while the act may be recognized as a crime, the motivation behind the act will be significant in identifying potential terrorists, engaging in appropriate investigation and ultimately apprehending the subject. Even the operational aspects are complicated. For example, it is one thing to apply standard techniques of hostage negotiation in a situation such as a bank robbery where the perpetrator primarily wanted to get the money and make a fast escape; it is an entirely different situation with a terrorist who engages in an act of violence not based on monetary gain. The act itself may be planned only to provoke a highly visible response by the police or military.

Even if there were agreement on a law-enforcement approach to terrorism, such an approach would stand in marked contrast to treating terrorism as a threat to national security and form of warfare. The complexity was best illustrated in the United States after the events of 9/11. Traditionally, within the legal system of the United States, domestic terrorism was treated as a criminal act. Consequently, on the national level, the Department of Justice would be responsible for addressing terrorism and would use the Federal Bureau of Investigation as its lead law-enforcement agency. As such, the focus would be on collection of evidence that would be used in court to prosecute those accused of threats or acts of terrorism. While such collections could be used in apprehending and trying those conspiring and engaging in terrorism, the main focus of the system would be terrorism as a criminal act. Because of this, the approach to combating terrorism would be largely reactive and after the fact. A more offensive approach, unfortunately, creates difficulties for democratic systems trying to address the threat.

While the use of preventative detention may enable authorities to seize a suspect in the short term, there are concerns that such actions violate civil liberties and due process. If taken to an extreme, these actions may be seen as a form of state repression that is commonly found in authoritarian governments. Another difficulty is the idea that if terrorism is treated as a crime, especially in a democratic system, the accused terrorist should be entitled to the same safeguards and rights as those who are accused of ordinary crimes. These include the basic rights against self-incrimination, the requirement for due process and protection of civil liberties and the requirement that the accused be able to confront their accusers in an open court. Those who wish to expand the capability to convict terrorists increasingly challenge these rights.

While it might be appropriate for the accused to confront their accusers, there is concern that the exposure of a source could not only reveal their sources and methods, but complicate the ability to take initiative against terrorists. The contention is based on the fact that the standard to collect evidence for legal action is higher than the standard to acquire information for intelligence and military operations where traditional safeguards and due process may not apply. In an ideal democratic system, the police primarily react to criminal behavior and, when confronted with violence, apply only minimum force where necessary. In contrast, if an act is defined in the context of warfare, the military becomes involved and a transformation from reactive to offensive takes place where the maximum use of force may be deemed appropriate.

In the past, one could contend that the law-enforcement approach was primarily used in regard to domestic acts, while a national-security, military or intelligence approach was accepted in conducting business overseas. The current problem is that the lines are becoming blurred. We are now witnessing what John O'Neill referred to as "seamless terrorism," which can be both domestic and international.[13] If a foreign group plans and is supported in the conduct of operations in one state to conduct operations in another, are we dealing with a criminal act, an act of armed hostility or an act of war?

Even before the events of 9/11, we witnessed profound changes in both the law-enforcement community and the military services. Police became heavily armed and increased their ability to engage in military operations, while the military has been barred from actively being involved in law-enforcement except in support roles. The military is also now being heavily relied upon for homeland rather than national security. We have therefore seen a change in the military, modeled similarly after national police forces with military capabilities and the militarization of the police, with the creation and use of highly trained tactical teams with counter-terrorism capabilities.

The seamless nature of terrorism is creating other challenges in regard to the role of intelligence. In the United States, the Central Intelligence Agency, which has been legally restricted from engaging in domestic intelligence, is now working closely with the Federal Bureau of Investigation. Conversely, the Federal Bureau of Investigation is increasingly being involved in the collection of international intelligence.

As a final note, with regard to the aforementioned corporate warriors, the corporate and private sector is a challenging and fast-paced environment that has often surpassed the government's ability to combat terrorism. We now see a massive emphasis on defense spending in non-governmental hands, resulting in the accountability of its uses not being as restricted as in the oversight process of governmental agencies.

In sum, while terrorism is a crime, a manifestation of the changing nature of conflict and a form of warfare to governments and academics, the victims and their families need not define it.

Terrorism as an Evolutionary Process

In a sense, terrorists are like sharks that must keep swimming if they are to receive the oxygen they need to survive. As will be seen in the next chapter, there is continuity in the strategy and nature of terrorism. The process can be appreciated by understanding the development of doctrine, which can be applied to understanding the evolution of terrorism.

There is fundamental doctrine that transcends time and there is environmental doctrine affected by gradual and profound changes in the political, social, economic, religious and especially the technological environments. Changes in any of these can cause new opportunities and dangers for terrorists. Finally, there is operational doctrine, the art and science of engaging in the carnage of terrorism. While doctrine does not offer a cognitive road map of future developments, it does provide a guide to identifying and evaluating future threats.[14] It bears repetition that terrorism is not mindless violence. It is not a happening; it is not the product of individuals and groups running amok. Therefore, in assessing the past, present and future of terrorism, the following axioms can help us to understand terrorism as an ongoing process.

At the outset, terrorists must adapt to what their available resources are. They traditionally are in a weaker position than their adversary – unless they are engaged in terrorism from above or regime repression. They must not only do more with less, they must also have the imagination to outmaneuver a stronger foe. As we have noted, they have an advantage over the cumbersome, large, inflexible militaries they face. In far too many cases, bureaucratic imagination is lacking and creativity is contradictory in terms. Terrorists must also adhere to the organizational and operational mantra that "small is beautiful." The small size of terrorist organizations circumvents their liability against a much larger adversary and turns it into an asset.

Neither terrorists nor their targets can afford to fail. The authorities of the targeted government are faced with the near-impossible task of preventing all terrorist incidents. One major incident can be traumatic, whereas success against terrorists is ironically marked when nothing happens. In the same manner, terrorist organizations in their early organizational phase cannot afford mistakes. Given their weak position and minimal resources, one error can be fatal. As with all other people, terrorists must learn from their mistakes if they are to survive. But, while terrorists often portray themselves as being revolutionary or on the cutting edge of political and societal change, they can also be caught in their own dogma and their own prisms of belief.

Conclusion

While one realizes the power of images in the media and the sense of fear they can create, the fact of the matter is that few people will directly experience the anguish of terrorism. I do not mean to minimize the profound physical and emotional cost to the victims and to their families and friends, but it remains that the ability of the terrorists to instill fear in a larger audience makes their actions so effective. And, as noted earlier, if people move beyond the routine precautions and profoundly alter their lives as a result of a loss of security, they have fallen into the trap of fear as intended by the terrorists. It is also important not to understate the threat and enter a stage of denial. A balance must be established.

This balance can be established by increasing one's understanding of terrorism. Terrorism is not mindless violence. Whether it is a tactic or strategy, a form of psychological warfare, a political weapon, a new form of warfare or a criminal act, it is not a monster that lurks in the dark, nor a monster that we can do nothing about. Understanding terrorism can help negate the fear that accompanies the sense of dread that comes from what we don't know. An understanding of terrorism can help us – and those responsible for providing our security – to avoid the ultimate threat: terrorizing ourselves.

–2–

Terrorism

A Historical Perspective

It is difficult to trace the origins and history of terrorism because it is so deeply embedded in the human experience. The fear of the unknown exists and creates terror where it cannot be explained in rational terms. Terror, in many instances, is generated by myth where dangers lurk in a universe of spirits, devils, monsters and other creations of the unique human imagination. To this day, children in their beds replicate this curse and blessing by creating their own threatening environment of things that go bump in the night.

Terrorism emerged when individuals and groups consciously exploited fear to influence the values and behaviors of others. This exploitation took place when the shaman, priest or other spiritual leaders maintained control by warning of how departure from the beliefs could lead to unimaginable terror in this life or the next. From the origins of religious belief to the Crusades to the Holy Terror of contemporary fundamentalism, fear and terror have often driven both victims and perpetrators of terrorism.

While the line between religious and secular terrorism has been and remains blurred, authorities tend to agree that it was the premeditated use of terror to achieve political goals that can be referred to as "ancient terrorism." In the long history of conflict and warfare, figures of authority have used terrorism to instill fear in enemies and enforce compliance from their followers.

The threat of fear and the use of violence were accepted as central aspects of conquest and control. A reputation for violence by the Tartars, the Huns, the Romans and barbarians was a legitimate aspect of warfare and the political life of the time. Great leaders, both famous and infamous, practiced their own forms of terrorism from above with the spear, the ax and the sword. But the evolution of modern terrorism can be seen particularly in the tactics of the following groups from the history of terrorism. They were innovators in the art of terrorism and their legacy remains today.

One of the first groups to use terrorism systematically as a weapon were the Zealots, Jewish nationalists in the first century CE who engaged in terrorists attacks against whom they viewed to be the Roman occupiers of Judea. Their attacks were directed against Roman officials – an example of targeting government representatives and a common tactic today. In addition they would kill those who were perceived to be Roman collaborators. Particularly significant was their use of the dagger in broad daylight, not only because it was effective, but also because it was an early form of psychological warfare where no one walking the streets could feel secure. This early form of intimidation was couple with another technique that has become a part of contemporary terrorism – ransoms. When their campaign ultimately failed, the survivors of the organization committed suicide at the Masada rather than be taken captive.

Another early group provided the origin of the term "assassin." These were the Shiite Muslims who, between the eighth and fourteenth centuries CE, sought their politico-religious objectives throughout the Middle East by having a small secret society of highly dedicated members who used daggers as their weapon of choice. While not clear whether it was a charge made by their adversaries or a fact, the assassins would engage in their acts of murder while high from the effects of *hashish*. The term assassin is derived from *hashshashin*. This group's use of extreme secrecy and long-term commitment to its cause has been the inspiration and legacy of contemporary groups such as Islamic Jihad.

Another group which provided the origin for a word – *thug* – now used to describe those engaged in common criminal behavior, has a more sinister beginning. The Thugs in both India and Asia, operating from the thirteenth to nineteenth centuries CE, were organizations of assassins who would often use a silk scarf to strangle their victims as the calling card of their activities. While they had a religious base, the Thugs hold a particular significance to contemporary terrorists in that they were professionals for hire. In a sense, they were precursors to the apolitical terrorists who engage in terrorism as an aspect of criminal activities that range from extortion to smuggling.[1]

While there were numerous groups that laid the foundation for contemporary terrorism, one of the earliest revolutionary groups was the *Narodnaya Volya* ("Peoples' Will" in English). In the late nineteenth century, they engaged in a wide variety of terrorists acts ranging from assassination to suicide bombing against officials in tsarist Russia. What was particularly striking about this group was that they specifically sought to avoid the killing of innocent bystanders. They also deliberately called themselves terrorists as opposed to freedom fighters, believing that the former was justified by a higher morality held in their battle against the oppressive state. The Russian terrorists of the time were dedicated to the principles of Sergei Nechaev, whose *Catechism of a Revolutionary* is a manual for terrorism that would be the antecedent for more recent guides, including Carlos Marighella's *Mini-Manual of the Urban Guerrilla*, the writings of Che Guevara and Regis Debray and the more technologically sophisticated manuals that can be found on the Internet.[2]

The Origins of the Age of Modern Terrorism

The emergence of modern terrorism was very much the product of the development of the nation-state. Until then, while terrorism was an integral aspect of political and social life, one did not view terrorism as a strategy or technique used to create or enforce order in a community nor as a means of transforming or destroying it. Until the beginning of the nation-state, there was not the contemporary concept of order defined in terms of the relations between sovereign nation-states necessitated by diplomacy, war or the combination of both. Even the initial creation of the state system did not create the conditions needed for the development of modern terrorism. A sovereign who may have used a degree of terrorism from above to guarantee the compliance of its subjects ruled the early states. These subjects did not view themselves to be part of the system, let alone to have an involvement in the politics of the court. Such involvement was also not necessary to legitimize the sovereign who generally ruled by divine right. All of that changed as a result of epochal events that took place during the American Revolutionary War. The concept of revolution – a product of the Enlightenment – maintained that a state could not be legitimate unless it represented the community of the nation. Nation, as defined by one authority, is

> a community of people who feel that they belong together in the double sense that they share deeply significant elements of a common heritage and that they have a common destiny in the future ... The nation is today the largest community which when the chips are down effectively command men's loyalty, overriding the claims of lesser communities within it and those which cut across it or potentially enfold it within a greater society reaching ultimately to mankind as a whole. In this sense the nation may be called a 'terminal community' with the implication that it is for the present purposes the effective end of the road for man as a social animal, the end point of the working solidarity between men. The nation has in fact become the body that legitimizes the state.[3]

The culmination of this concept, which was rooted in a democratic ideal of government, also marked the beginning of the age of modern terrorism with the onset of the French Revolution. On one hand, this revolution maintained that the legitimacy of a state could not be justified on the basis of divine right, but only on the basis that the state represented a particular community known as a nation through a concept of democratic government. On the other hand, however, this revolution spawned the phrase "reign of terror," which was viewed as not only an acceptable but positive means by which the revolutionary government could restore order after the chaotic period of revolutionary activities. It was this requirement for order that led to the development of state terrorism. *Le Comité de Salut Public* (the Committee of Public Safety), under the rule of Maximilien Robespierre, was the de facto executive government of France during this reign of terror. From September 5, 1793 until the summer of 1794, estimated numbers ranging between 18,000 and 40,000 people were executed for being adjudged enemies of the state. The reign of terror was followed by other great purges which culminated in genocide and the events of the French Revolution marked the use of the word "terror" as a clearly identifiable aspect of political life.

The profound impact of the French Revolution in the creation of modern terrorism and the ongoing calls for self-determination by those who seek their own national identity remains a very salient aspect of the causes of contemporary terrorism, just as the response to such terrorism has continued to be state terrorism. While the legacy of that revolution remains, there are two significant changes: first, the development of terrorism which goes beyond the call for self-determination in the context of a nation-state and, secondly, the emergence of non-state actors who challenge the primacy of the nation-state system in contemporary international affairs.

Modern Terrorism

As noted earlier, while terrorism may be as old as or even older than recorded history, contemporary terrorism is the result of global changes, a few of which will be discussed below.

Modern terrorism is a manifestation of the rise of non-state actors in international affairs. Just as the French Revolution is used as the origin of modern terrorism based on the establishment of the modern nation-state system, based on the concept of legitimacy, based on community, ironically so has contemporary terrorism become a manifestation of the rise of non-state actors in the international arena. Increasingly the traditional state-centric system that was affirmed by the Treaty of Westphalia has been challenged by universal and regional intergovernmental organizations, trans-national guerrilla and terrorist groups and a growing number of nongovernmental organizations that function in varying areas of the international arena.[4] One could also add multinational corporations who traditionally have been highly symbolic and lucrative targets of terrorist acts and campaigns and organized criminal enterprises.

While the primacy of the nation-state is now being challenged, it must be noted that the motivation to engage in terrorism under the banner of self-determination remains a major characteristic of current conflict as a result of arbitrary boundaries dating back to the colonial period, the release of suppressed national sentiments held in check during the Cold War by a repressive Soviet Union and the reassertion of traditional ethnic, language and religious values with the often accompanying demand by secessionist move-ments. The challenge to the existing nation-system has further been exacerbated by another significant factor, namely the break-down of the coercive power of the sate and the consequent blurring of the line between public force and private violence. This break-down has serious implications not only in regard to the capabilities and goals of the terrorists but to the governments and increasingly other entities seeking to counter the terrorist threat. We are now witnessing the privatization of public violence that may be one of the hallmarks to what will later be discussed as an aspect of contemporary and future trends of terrorism.[5]

The current change in modern terrorism is also a manifestation of yet another change – that is, it can be maintained that contem-porary terrorism is a new form of the diplomatic method. This is not to suggest that the trend has no historical antecedents. The terms "gun-boat diplomacy" and its more contemporary and semantically refined equivalent "coercive diplomacy" have regu-larly been used by nation-states to achieve their objectives. There are differences that, while having continuity with the past, serve to underscore characteristics of modern terrorism.

At the outset, there are increasing numbers of states that have rejected the traditional diplomatic method as a means of conducting their relations with other states. In fact, in a number of instances this rejection is based on a view that the nation-state was and is essentially the product of Western imperial powers and the means by which they maintained their global domination in the past centuries. The so-called rules of the game are not viewed to be part of the execution of foreign policy.

This again does not mean to suggest that states practicing traditional diplomacy do not resort to war in the pursuit of the objectives, but that states not accepting norms such as diplomatic immunity and the major edicts of international law are loathe to work within the system. Indeed, these states thrive on confrontation based on ideological or religious grounds that are often fed by xenophobia. Taken to the extreme, we have what have been called "rogue states." While such states have certainly existed in the past, they pose in our time a major threat to national, regional and international security since they increasingly have the capability to develop or acquire a wide variety of weapons of mass destruction. Even the most paranoid of states in the past lacked this capability. In the pursuit of their objectives, these states are quite willing to employ terrorism as a form of their own diplomatic method, in which an exchange of bullets replaces the exchange of ambassadors and the presentation of a letter of credence by a new ambassador to a head of state is supplanted by the taking hostage of embassy personnel. Equally troubling is the fact that these "terror states" often terrorize their own people as well as outsiders and appear more than willing to engage in the support of a wide variety of terrorist groups. Such countries as North Korea have effectively utilized the support of terrorist groups and the possible capability of providing them with weapons of mass destruction to engage in what is essentially diplomatic blackmail. Finally, we have witnessed the merging of failed states which are located in the gray area of nations, immense regions where control has shifted from legitimate governments to new half-political, half-criminal powers.[6]

In these areas terrorists and criminals control large areas and may be funded from the cultivation and sale of drugs, in an area where a government cannot assert its power or simply does not exist. In the gray area, terrorists have the sanctuaries and base of operations to conduct global operations whether it be from the tri-border area in Latin America or the border between Afghanistan and Pakistan. Furthermore, criminal gangs have not only become significant in the international arena, but have, as in the case of the South Malaccans, humbled a superpower which, after engaging in humanitarian programs, sought to defeat warlords who played by their own rules.

The resort to terrorism as an aspect of what can be called a new diplomatic method is also a manifestation of a new form of warfare. Ultimately, terrorism is an integral aspect of a transformation not only in warfare, but in other forms of physical conflict and violence as well. As we shall see, it has created challenges to conventional military thinking, strategy and tactics and has created a conflict environment in which now not only national militaries and their police forces wield power, but also corporate and other groups must be contended with. Nation-states must now adjust to a new reality resulting from a motivation on the part of adversaries which may be based on the reassertion of traditional values and a desire to return to an idealized past, but which also may lead those adversaries to not hesitate to use the most modern weaponry to achieve their goals.

Conclusion

In the final analysis, the emergence of modern terrorism, its major characteristics, goals, strategies, tactics and future can only be understood in the context of the profound impact of globalization and the conflicting forces that make it such a complex issue. What we are witnessing is the assertion of traditional values in an expanding technological and informational universe. That is, the very technology and especially the information on the world-wide-web, that has penetrated the increasingly porous, imaginary boundary of the nation-state, has created a reaction on the part of people who are seeking to redefine themselves on more traditional lines.

This sense of community and reassertion of values can lead to secessionist movements, such as those in Chechnya, Sri Lanka or the Basque region of Spain, that utilize terrorism as the primary method for reestablishing their identities. Yet, at the same time, this quest for community goes beyond the boundaries of existing nation-states as various groups impelled by their values and beliefs seek a sense of community that is regional – and indeed, global – in nature. The assertion of Islamic fundamentalism and those who have interpreted it to justify their resort to terrorism is a profound illustration that communities can resort to terrorism as a means of not only contracting their "terminal community" but at other times expanding it beyond the nation-state. In this quest for parochial and transnational communities that are in many instances a symptom of reaction against and rejection of the mass secular industrialized and postindustrial societies, especially the United States, technology has increasingly become the weapon of choice by those who would go "back to the future". The weapons that are being used are not limited to more sophisticated hand-held weapons of mass destruction. For what we are now witnessing is the chilling fact that terrorists are effectively utilizing the information revolution to advance their goals through what is now known as "social netwar." The profound impact of netwar, not only operationally but organizationally, will be discussed in detail in chapter 6. The implications of such a form of terrorism will have serious impacts on how authorities on all levels, within both public and private sectors, will have to adjust to a new form of diplomacy and a new form of warfare.

–3–

The Rationale of Terror

While it may be emotionally difficult to conceive of terrorism as a form of purposeful violence when one sees the shocking results of such acts, the fact remains that terrorism is "violence for effect." Despite the horrendous images of carnage especially directed against civilians, terrorism is goal-directed. For example, while the target could be a building for its symbolic value or a government official because he or she represents the power of the state, the goal is to affect the audience – the public witnessing the attack. While it is difficult for the family of the victim to have suffered a loss, the ultimate target of the terrorists is often the government and the citizens writ large of the country being attacked. The greatest effect, however, is intended to be upon the audience who can use public opinion to push the government into giving the terrorist organization what it wants. It is a tragic reality that the more senseless an attack may be to the public, the more sense it makes to the terrorists as a means of enhancing the trauma of a stunned audience.

While a particular perpetrator may be mentally unstable, most violent acts of terrorism are rational and, whether one wishes to accept it or not, most individuals who engage in such violence are not mentally disturbed. Acceptance of this fact is not easy, especially since such a judgment may appear to justify acts of carnage. But, this recognition of rationality does not mean to imply that the act has some form of legitimacy. Rather, acceptance of the purposeful and instrumental nature of terrorism provides the basis to understand the act and not simply react to it emotionally. Furthermore, to understand the act is to provide the foundation for recognizing the goals, strategies and tactics of terrorism and developing the ability to predict future incidents, to understand why they are taking place and – ideally – to prevent, deter or prepare to respond effectively both as individuals and as a community when such an act takes place.

If terrorism were mindless violence, if it were not purposeful, if it were a happening, how could one understand and therefore counter terrorism? If these were so, those terrorists would be involved in often spontaneous, unplanned and essentially random acts of violence driven by mental illness and inner demons. In effect, an understanding of the rationality of terrorism, however repugnant the act may be, provides the analytical capability that can enable us to cope with the event instead of reacting emotionally, possibly resulting in an overreactive response to the next threat, incident or terrorist campaign.

This chapter will be an overview providing the basis for a more specific discussion of the other major characteristics of terrorism. For this chapter, I will utilize various illustrations of terrorism to show its purposeful nature.

While terrorism is not irrelative to the immediate victim or their family and friends, the magnitude of terrorism cannot be measured on the basis of an obscene body count. Furthermore, while acts of terrorism are often tactical in nature, they may be part of a strategic objective and result in a profound impact beyond the immediate area of the act and its victims.

At the inception of modern terrorism, the attacks, no matter how dramatic, were not viewed as having a regionally, much less global, geopolitical impact. Despite the fact that acts might be accorded international attention, they were not regarded as having global significance because to many governments and individuals terrorism was what happened to other people in other places. Even the publications of such a highly regarded organization as the International Institute for Strategic Studies, which covered terrorism, did not initially regard it as an element that could alter the geopolitical landscape. In the United States, that insularity changed with the bombing in Oklahoma City, OK, the heartland of the

United States and changed even more so following the events of 9/11. It was finally realized that no country, no matter how powerful, was immune from the emergence of terrorism on its shores. Yet, there had been many incidents before those events which served to underscore that acts of terrorism could be both tactical and strategic in the broadest context of international security and relations and that such acts could have both short- and long-term impacts. The following illustrations briefly present the purposeful nature of terrorism at all levels, ranging from the impact on the individual to decision-making at the highest policy level.

While the September 5, 1972 Munich Massacre has often been viewed to be the act inaugurating the age of modern terrorism, there was an earlier act on May 30 of that same year which illustrates aspects of the purposeful nature of terrorism – purposes that are still being sought by the latest generation of terrorists. On that date, three members of the Japanese Red Army (JRA) killed twenty-five civilians, including Puerto Rican pilgrims and injured seventy-six when they opened fire inside the Lod Airport in Tel Aviv, Israel.

Their act serves to underscore that while terrorism is purposeful, those who engage in it may have very mixed reasons for their acts and this type of case raises vexing problems related to the ultimate purpose of the individuals who engaged in this act of carnage. At the outset, it is difficult to label the ideological objectives of the JRA clearly. On one hand, they appear to be extremely violent members of a rather diffuse leftist anarchist movement who denounced "Western imperialism" and would use terrorism as an instrument to achieve a vague goal of creating a Japanese People's Republic. Yet the outward commitment to an ideology was blurred by the internal purges in the early 1970s which led to the death of a number of its members. The reasons for the purge are by no means clear, but serve to underscore the fact that in this case of the JRA, the line between mystical cult behavior and purposeful political acts was at the very least blurred. The confusion was perhaps best verbalized by the sole surviving member of the team that conducted the attack, Kozo Okamoto. At one point he stated that upon his death he would become a shooting star and yet at another time he stated that "the only drugs for us are Marxist Leninism. The world of Che Guevara is the only stimulus we need."[1] Despite the lack of a clearly defined ideology and perhaps because of it, the members of JRA were known as "ideological mercenaries" who were willing to hire themselves out to more conventional groups such as the General Command of the Popular Front for the Liberation of Palestine. Their willingness to literally be guns for hire to other terrorist organizations is illustrated by attacks on US and British embassies in Rome and the attack on a US Servicemen's club in Rome. These attacks were probably sponsored by Libya as retaliation for the US raid on Libya in 1986 for Operation El Dorado Canyon, which was in response to the bombing of a Berlin disco where American personnel were among the five killed and two hundred wounded. Even into the 1980s and 1990s, this strange group remained active with the rocketing of US, Canadian and Japanese embassies in 1986 and attacks on the Imperial Palaces in Tokyo and Japan in January 1990. The long life of the JRA is perhaps best illustrated in that it took thirty-one years to finally bring one of the original leaders to justice – Ms. Fusako Shigenobu – in November 2000. Some members still remain at large.

The short-term impact of the Lod Airport massacre as a precursor to Munich was that of a warning shot not only to Israel, but to the rest of the world, that aviation was a prime target for future terrorists' attacks. Israel learned from the painful lesson of the Lod Airport massacre, but also earlier attacks, most notably the ones occurring during September 6–9, 1970 in which the Popular Front for the Liberation of Palestine hijacked five commercial airliners and held hostage 400 passengers and crew. From these lessons, Israel became preeminent in the field of aviation security. Also in the short term, the JRA effectively engaged in purposeful economic warfare by discouraging tourism in Israel. As one of the perpetrators said, any tourist was guilty because they came to Israel. It is perhaps the long-term impact of the Lod Airport massacre and the other actions of the JRA that are particularly troublesome today. The JRA activities underscored the fact that even if terrorist groups had different purposes and goals, they could work together in a murderous marriage of convenience via joint training and coordinated attacks. This was discovered long before the emergence of Al Qaeda.

Perhaps the first major incident that introduced the American public to terrorism was the seizure of the US embassy in Tehran, Iran on November 4, 1979. This 444-day hostage situation aptly illustrates how terrorism can be used to achieve a wide range of purposes, from creating an emotional involvement of the citizens and leaders of a country to achieving a profound impact on the election of a country's President. As noted early on in the period of the incident, "America was held hostage."

The hostage taking was not spontaneous but well planned and executed. The execution and anticipated outcome of the act had multiple purposes, all of which, to a large degree, were realized. First, while ostensible "students" seized the embassy, it was in cooperation with the political leadership of the Iranian government. The event was, in effect, a form of state-sanctioned hostage taking. By emphasizing the role of the students, the government was able to engage in what is called plausible deniability and claim that they were not involved. Secondly, the incident provided an opportunity for the hostage-takers to use the mass media very skillfully to justify their actions by their critique of the US government, especially in reference to how the Central Intelligence Agency conducted a campaign of political subversion that led to the downfall of Mohammed Mossadegh, who had attempted to nationalize the British-owned Anglo-Iranian Oil Company and replaced him with the Shah in August 1953. The United States was also blamed for providing the funding and advice that enabled the internal security service – the Savak – to engage in its own form of regime repression through the use of torture. In this manner, the hostage-takers were successful in not only dramatizing their cause, but engaging in "guilt transfer" by "blaming the victim" (in this case the US and its detained embassy personnel). But, what was particularly interesting in the realm of an international incident was the ability of the hostage-takers to effectively play on the sensitivities of the American public and, in doing so, create a long-term "soap opera". A massive audience listened to reports on the progress (or lack thereof) each night. The hostage-takers were able to keep such an attentive audience because the viewers were able to relate to the families of the hostages. Unlike a mass incident, the hostages became reluctant media personalities as their families effectively pressured the government to seek their release.

While an immediate incident of massive terrorism with a large number of casualties is tragic, hostages being held in captivity for an extended period of time can bring about more emotions and a stronger ability for the public to relate to the victims. However, this changed with the Oklahoma City bombing on April 19, 1995 and the change was even more obvious after 9/11. These events created a sense of shared loss held by a national community in the weeks and months following these tragedies. However, they both lacked the continuous dramatic appeal of relating to a group of recognizable, living victims on a daily basis. The Iranian government and the mass media further heightened this dramatic impact. The government acted through the students and was able to take a hard line or suggest that negotiations were working, effectively creating an emotional rollercoaster for the 444 days of the hostage negotiations. Moreover, the press would "leak" stories to heighten the drama and keep the television ratings high when there was a potential weakening interest. At the same time, Washington could also provide different interpretations in pursuits of different political agendas. This is especially significant because the Iranians knew that public opinion was both the strength and the weakness of the American democratic system. They knew how to take advantage of this and purposefully played with it, especially after the abortive rescue attempt of Desert One executed on April 24, 1980, resulting in the death of several servicemen and a great amount of embarrassment to the United States. This operation severely discredited President Carter's leadership and, along with previous failures to resolve the hostage incident, played well into the hands of Ronald Reagan, who used the hostage situation as one of the means to deride the Carter administration. Reagan was then elected President on his credit as "The Great Communicator." It was not ironic that the freedom of the hostages would take place at the end of one administration and the start of another. For all intents and purposes, the hostage-taking enabled the Iranian government and its "students" to have a direct impact on the election in the country they regarded as "The Great Satan."

Even more immediate effects of terrorist attacks can be seen in looking at the bombing of the Madrid subway on March 11, 2004. The attack not only affected the outcome of their elections, but changed a very crucial aspect of Spain's foreign policy – the withdrawal of its troops from Iraq. One can anticipate that the bomb and the bullet will be used again as a means of purposefully intruding into the electoral process of other states. In a real sense, the terrorists have learned from their experience that the bullet may be as effective as the ballot box in determining how people will vote. Terrorists have also learned that the exchange of bullets may be even more effective than the exchange of ambassadors. Armed diplomacy – that is, diplomacy by the gun – has become an alternative form of diplomacy. The purposeful use of public opinion to test the resolve of a people, a nation and the international community will be discussed in more detail in chapter 5.

Another dramatic and effective terrorist attack in the earlier history of contemporary terrorism occurred at 6:20 a.m. on October 23, 1983. The bombing of the US Marine Peacekeeping barracks in Beirut, Lebanon resulted in 241 fatalities and eighty-one injuries. Moments later, another bombing took place at the buildings housing the French peacekeeping troops, which resulted in another fifty-nine fatalities and fifteen more injuries. The attack on the Marines showed that the attackers viewed them as combatants in an ongoing war and not the peacekeepers they claimed to be. This reason, however, did not lessen the pain and anguish of the families who lost their loved ones – whether or not they were viewed as noncombatants or combatants.

The act served to underscore the ability of the terrorists to frame the incident purposefully as a means of pursuing their agenda. That is, the marines were a target of warfare and not a target of opportunity. The terrorists made the case that they and the US forces were involved in an ongoing war, not a condition of armed conflict in an environment of neither war nor peace. The pro-Iranian Shiite Moslem group known as Hezbollah, the "Party of God," not only provided a basis to legitimize their actions as part of an ongoing armed conflict, but also put Washington on notice that with the additional attack on French quarters, they were attacking as a form of warfare and not a campaign of terrorism. Washington did not respond by declaring official war against the terrorists and their sponsors.

Whether one agrees or not, the terrorists framed their actions in such a way as to achieve a degree of legitimacy, if not with the United States and its allies then with those governments and organizations that viewed the action to be an acceptable response to the placement of US troops in Lebanon. The perpetrators of the attack did not view the peacekeepers as such despite the claims of Washington. They viewed the placement of US troops in their country as a way for Washington to impose its policy of a pro-American Lebanese government. This event was especially significant because the terrorists were successful in achieving their purposeful, strategic objective: Hezbollah, a terrorist group, effectively created the conditions that led to ousting one of the world's superpowers and its allies from Lebanon. In the short term, the attacks achieved the objective of putting Washington's policy in disarray. In the long term, it demonstrated that acts of terrorism, if skillfully planned and conducted have the potential of altering foreign policies without resorting to diplomatic methods or a war with a clearly defeated enemy.

Since these incidents, terrorists have continuously refined their ability to engage in purposeful violence in order to dramatize their causes, to coerce a mass public to listen to their message, to engage in economic warfare and to directly intrude on the outcome of other countries' elections and subsequent changes in policy. Perhaps most significant of all is that terrorists, through both individual attacks and campaigns of terrorism, are purposefully seeking to engage in what they hope will become a self-fulfilling prophecy – that is, they claim that the democratic, largely secular states of the West are ultimately repressive. Terrorists view these states as supporting repressive regimes that desire to maintain their economic and political dominance in this age of globalization. More specifically, terrorists are attempting to create the conditions by which these democratic governments begin repressing their own citizens. There is nothing new in the use of this prophecy from past experiences – one difference, however, is that historically it was directed toward a specific government, but now it is international in scope. One of the best illustrations of the self-fulfilling prophecy is that of Uruguay and their experience with Tupamaros. There are lessons about democratization to be learned from that small Latin American state.

In the context of the time in the 1960s and early 1970s, Uruguay was a functioning democratic state. Starting in 1973 it experienced incidents of urban terrorism conducted by the leftist guerrilla group the Uruguayan Movimiento de Liberación Nacional (MLN) which sought to expel foreign economic and political interests. The group was commonly referred to as the Tupamaros, named after an Inca leader who was executed by the Spanish. As in the case of other Latin American terrorists, it engaged in bombings and bank robberies. The latter was based on the tactics employed by the Brazilian Carlos Marighella whose book, *The Mini-Manual of the Urban Guerrilla*, became required reading for Latin American, American and European terrorists, who used his bank-robbery technique as means of raising funds for the cause.[2] The Tupamaros did engage in two early kidnappings that were international in character – one, in 1971, was of Daniel A. Mitione, a US Agency for International Development official who was advising local law enforcement. The incident ended with his murder. In a second case, the British Ambassador Geoffrey Jackson was kidnapped and released. His book, *Surviving the Long Night*, should be required reading for those who want to know how an individual maintained his dignity and leadership position even while he was in a "People's Prison."[3] The national tragedy for the people and government was played out when the MLN targeted police and security forces who responded by declaring an internal war against the terrorist. Tactically, the government achieved a victory: they destroyed the Tupamaros. But, it was a pyrrhic victory because the security forces also destroyed the democratic system – martial law was declared and a military junta took power. Thus, the prophecy was realized – the terrorists claimed the government was repressive, took actions to cause an overreaction and as a result, the government became what the terrorists wished it would be.

There are very important lessons to be gleaned from this experience given today's events. The terrorists are now intentionally targeting newly formed and often fragile democratic orders by employing provocative acts to create an overreaction by the government. Such examples include the quick passage of the USA Patriot Act in the United States after 9/11 and the challenges of reconciling civil liberties and secularism with the rise of traditional Islamic practices. The classic issue of engaging on personal, national and international levels in the delicate balance between security and civil liberties is a major challenge. Security must be reconciled without succumbing to paranoia and allowing the erosion of due process or the emergence of domestic and transnational surveillance societies where privacy is no longer protected.

A Word of Caution: The Danger of Ascribing too Much Purposefulness to Incidents of Violence

While it is important to understand that terrorism can be viewed as a purposeful form of violence and that such an understanding can help us not emotionally react to what appears to be mindless violence, one should also appreciate that while a rational approach to terrorism may bring analytical order from what appears to be purposeless violence the approach cannot possibly explain all of the motivation behind the use of terrorism.

On the level of individual behavior, as noted earlier, there are and will be people who resort to terrorism for reasons either unrelated or distantly related to the acts. For others, terrorism may be used to cover up their most primal emotions driven by factors such as a real or perceived threat to survival or a desire for revenge. These emotions may be the result of any number of psychological considerations that range from what could be regarded as normal behavior when confronted by a threat to abnormal behavior based on some psychological disorder. But, whatever the cause, it must be kept in mind that while there might be underlying, precipitating and accelerating reasons for which individuals engage in violent acts of terrorism, it is important to understand that terrorism creates its own dynamic. The reason for an individual engaging in terrorism may not be the result of his or her political or religious beliefs. Rather, they may be driven by anything ranging from revenge to blood feuds to fear of strangers or to countless other elements that may cause fear of "the others."

It would be so much easier if we could identify underlying causes, eliminating them and ideally negating the need for terrorism as a purposeful action. Unfortunately, where violence in the form of terrorism is present a self-perpetuating cycle of terrorism and counterterrorism can develop. This cycle is fueled by individual anger and a desire to strike back or a government's declared aim to protect public security and preserve its legitimacy as the holder of the monopoly of power that characterizes a state and its concept of sovereignty.

How the cycle of violence can be broken is beyond the scope and the abilities of this book and myself. The key may be education in its broadest sense. As Lieutenant Cable said in his song in the musical *South Pacific*: "You got to be taught to be afraid of people whose skins is a different shade, it got to be drummed in your own little ear, you got to be carefully taught." How else does one explain a hatred that is so deep that it led to the death of four young girls at the Sixteenth Street Baptist Church in Birmingham, Alabama by members of the Ku Klux Klan on September 15, 1963?[4] How does one explain the murder of 330 individuals, almost half of them children, on September 3, 2004 by Chechen separatists in a school in Beslan, Russia? How far has the human condition really progressed in the forty-one years since that earlier act of terrorism? At what point does hatred lead to rage and rage to terrorism?

Whether one looks at the horrors of an individual murder or an act of mass terrorism, however purposeful the act may appear, one must also grapple with profound issues associated with questions of morality. Terrorism is a manifestation of evil that is just as real as the evil which terrorists associate with the groups and governments they target.

–4–

The Strategies and Tactics of Terrorism

The Abominable Art of Violence

Strategic Goals

As we have seen, those who resort to terrorism engage in purposeful violence, but the purpose is often far more than a generalized desire to instill fear and intimidation into the target audience. Rather, the violence may be an integral aspect of a strategy to advance the terrorists' causes systematically, whether such a cause is based on a secular ideology, a particular interpretation of religious doctrine or the unique mythology of a cult. Whatever the reason, an understanding of the strategy, be it general or specific, simplistic or complex, can enable us to understand the objectives of those who are engaging in their own form of armed conflict against nations, regions or indeed the entire global order. Moreover, an understanding of the strategy can help us to better appreciate the tactics that may be used to advance the strategy, tactics which can range from crude explosive devises to the increased threat of highly sophisticated forms of modern conventional and unconventional weapons of both selective and mass destruction. It is difficult to label groups by their strategies since, as we shall see, strategies may be the result of motivational factors ranging from the secular to the religious traditions or even a combination of both. Nevertheless, one can identify different goals forming the basis for and justification of, the resort to the tactics of terrorism.

At the outset, there have been those groups who have followed in the long tradition of anarchism that called for the total destruction of the existing political, economic and social order. Such individuals as Mikhail Bakunin, who sought to destroy the Czarist regime in Russia, emphasized that the resort to violence, as contrasted to rhetoric, was essential for destroying the old order. Perhaps the most chilling supporter of this view was Bakunin's colleague Sergei Nechaev, whose *Catechism of a Revolutionary* provides insights not only in regard to the dedication of an anarchist but to even those contemporary terrorists who have rejected society and look to violence to achieve their personal fulfillment. As he noted,

> The revolutionary is a doomed man. He has no interests of his own, no affairs, no attachments, no belongings, not even a name ... Everything in him is absorbed by a single thought, a single passion – the revolution ... The revolutionary enters into the world of the state, of the class, of so-called culture and lives in it only because he has faith in its speedy and total destruction. He is not a revolutionary if he feels pity for anything in this world. If he is able to he must face the annihilation of the situation – everything and everyone must be equally odious to him. All the worse to him if he has family and loved ones in the world: he is no revolutionary if he can stay his hand.[1]

While this statement was made by an anarchist, it is important to recognize that the level of dedication, the rejection of self and family and the commitment to violence is a fearful tradition that continues whether the terrorist be one of nineteen who hijacked aircraft on September 11, 2001 or the nameless suicide bomber who will engage in killing civilians, military personnel and police in Iraq, Sri Lanka or other areas in the Middle East and South and Southeast Asia.

The impact of the anarchist tradition in modern terrorism was particularly significant from the late 1960s to the 1980s, a period which saw a fusion of the tradition of anarchism and left-wing ideologies, with the emergence of campaigns of terrorism by anarcho-communists.[2] These groups, through their bombing, hostage-taking and kidnapping, posed a threat particularly in Western Europe. The Red Army Faction formerly known as the Baader-Meinhof Gang engaged in more than fifty-three actions from 1972 to 1991, including the attempted assassination of then NATO Commander General Alexander Haig in 1979, the assassination of various German officials and businessmen including the head of the Deutsche Bank, Alfred Herrhausen, in 1989 and attacks on US military personnel and installations. The Red Army Faction had its counterpart in Italy, the Red Brigades (*Brigate Rosse*), who also engaged in a series of terrorist campaigns which culminated with the kidnapping and death of Aldo Moro, the former Prime Minister of Italy, in 1978 and the kidnapping of General James Dozier (later successfully rescued) in 1981.

As in the case of other European anarchist groups, the strategy of both the Red Army Faction (RAF) and Red Brigades (RB) was ultimately very general in nature. They sought to destroy the existing capitalist system without providing any alternatives to replace it. Indeed, their writing often took the form of diatribes against the social and political order and in their own manner emphasized the need for action, as illustrated by the following statement:

> Comrades ... there is no point in trying to explain the right way to deceitful people. That we have done long enough. We don't have to explain Baader-Release Action to the intellectual prattlers ... the know-it-alls, but rather to the potentially revolutionary segment of the people. That means to those who can immediately grasp the deed, because they themselves are imprisoned. To those who think nothing of the prattle of the Left because it has remained without consequence or deeds. [In other words] those who have had enough.[3]

The stress on action instead of rhetoric followed much in the anarchist tradition of "propaganda by the deed." That is, "ideas result from the deeds, not the latter from the former." One could suggest therefore that to the RAF and to other European anarchist groups, violence in the 1970s and 1980s ultimately was not instrumental, but an end unto itself.[4]

As a result, one can suggest that while tactics were specifically to target people and facilities viewed to be symbols of a decadent old order, the strategy was very broad in scope. Consequently governments were faced with an adversary which did not provide them with a concrete strategic plan that could be analyzed and dealt with through effective counterterrorism measures. This problem remains today, as a wide variety of anarchist groups in their rejection of globalization lack a detailed and clearly enunciated strategy – that is, one which can be used by counterterrorists both to identify a strategy that clearly defines itself and to anticipate future acts or campaigns of terrorism.

If it is difficult to ascertain a well-defined strategy in regard to anarchist groups, it is even more difficult to understand the strategy – if one can call it that – of various sects or cults who have resorted to terrorism as a means of seeking to achieve their often macabre goals. Perhaps the best and most frightful group was Aum Shinrikyo, who by their actions initiated the age of modern mass terrorism with their sarin gas attack on the Tokyo subway system on March 20, 1995. The strategy was based on a very eclectic doomsday quasi-religion which combined the Hindu God of Destruction Shiva with the Judeo-Christian concept of Armageddon, some teachings of Yoga and the apocalyptic prophecies of Nostradamus. According to the leader of the cult, Shoko Ashara, his special reading of history would lead to the following:

> First ... trade frictions with the U.S. would cause Japan's standard of living to plummet in the 1990s and lead to a virtual police state. The year 1996 will "witness the sinking of Japan" – an evil land mass devoured in its entirety by waves. Then, in 1999, the end of the world begins. Early next century, Russia, China, the U.S. and Europe will collapse. In the year 2003 ... Armageddon will enter its final phase with a nuclear war that lays waste civilization. From the rubble of this post-apocalyptic world will rise a race of "superhumans," the followers of Shoko Ashara.[5]

This scenario attracted young, disaffected scientists and techni-
cians who saw in the writings and behavior of the charismatic
leader of the sect a means to bring purpose to their lives. More
ominously; it armed the cult with high technological capabilities to
engage in mass terrorism. While Ashara is now imprisoned and has
been sentenced to death and the cult has lost most of its influence,
its followers still are active in Japan, Russia and other locations.
However, perhaps even more troublesome is a realization that one
may see the rise of other cults much in the tradition of Aum which,
as a reaction to what they regard to be the evils of modernization,
globalization and other factors may pursue their own terrorist
agenda in the name of an exotic and dangerous strategic vision.
Moreover it is also important to recognize that individuals who
were, in a sense, a terrorist organization and cell of one, have also
represented a serious threat to public security and that like the
anarchist of the past their motivation may not be spiritual or religious in nature. Thus, for example, the Unabomber Theodore J.
Kaczynski was responsible for more than sixteen mailed parcel-
bomb attacks which killed three and maimed twenty-five others
from 1978 to 1985. His long and rambling diatribe against the
current technological order was readily available, even being
printed in the *New York Times*.

Like the Luddites of the nineteenth century who sought to stop
the industrial revolution by destroying the machines that made it
possible, Kaczynski attempted to stop a new and ever-accelerating
wave of technological development through his individual efforts.
As he stated:

> We therefore advocate a revolution against the industrial system. This
> revolution may or may not make use of violence: it may be sudden or
> it may be a relatively gradual process spanning a few decades. We can't
> predict any of that. But we do outline in a very general way the meas-
> ures that those who hate the industrial system should take in order to
> prepare a revolution against that form of society. This is not to be a
> political revolution. Its object will be to overthrow not governments but
> the economic and technological basis of the present society.[6]

The Unabomber of course lacked the capability to stem the change he railed against, but at the height of his actions he very effectively intimidated the public. One can wonder what additional disruption Kaczynski would have created if he'd been a member of a highly organized group of individuals who would use technology to destroy the technological order.

There are, however, major groups who through their interpretation of their religion have not only enunciated strategic goals, but have become important players in the international and regional arena as a result of their acts and campaigns of terrorism. Two representative groups are Hamas and Al Qaeda.

Hamas is an example of an exceedingly well organized group. It emerged from the Muslim Brotherhood in Egypt and was established in 1988. Its *Covenant of the Islamic Resistance Movement* called for the destruction of the state of Israel and establishment of a Palestinian state based on the principles of Islam. Now that a Palestinian state *has* been established, there is continual tension and competition between those who subscribe to a secular state based on Palestinian nationalism and Hamas who views nationalism as part and parcel of their religious faith and ultimately has as its goal the waging of Jihad in a Pan-Islamic context that includes not only the Middle East, but the rest of the globe as well.

Hamas received ideological inspiration from the Islamic revolution in Iran. The fundamentalist beliefs and goals are spelled out as follows:

> Hamas regards Nationalism (Wataniyya) as part and parcel of the religious faith. Nothing is loftier or deeper in waging Jihad against the enemy and confronting him when he sets foot on the land of Muslims … While other nationalisms consist of material, human and territorial considerations, the nationality of Hamas also carries, in addition to all of those, the all important divine factors which lead to spirit and life: so much so that it connects with the origins of the spirit and the source of life and raises in the skies of the Homeland the banner of the Lord, thus inexorably connecting earth with heaven.[7]

In Hamas we see the full development of non-territorial terrorism founded on religious beliefs and consciously operating within and beyond the boundaries of nation-states and the limitations of primarily pursuing nationalistic goals.

In the pursuit of its strategic goals Hamas has employed a whole plethora of tactics ranging from bombing to hijacking to kidnapping. But they have especially refined, with murderous efficiency, suicide bombing (martyrdom attacks) which they learned from Hezbollah operatives, when 400 Hamas radicals were exiled by the Israelis to Lebanon. Ironically, the tactic was put into practice when the Israeli government allowed many of the exiles to return with the erroneous assumption that they could use Hamas as a counterbalance to the Palestinian Liberation Organization and its supporters. (There is a lesson to be learned here about the danger of a government seeking to ride on the back of a tiger in the pursuit of its objectives. Washington faces a similar challenge in regard to determining what its relationship should be with Hezbollah, which is a major political force to be reckoned with in Lebanon.)

What is particularly significant about Hamas, as well as other terrorist organizations who have employed the same national-religious strategy, is the fact that through very extensive sponsorship of medical clinics, a whole host of social services and educational institutions ranging from kindergarten to universities, Hamas is filling the needs of individuals who have been ignored by what, under President Arafat, was probably one of the most corrupt governments in the world – the Palestinian Authority. These services gave Hamas not only a level of general support but also a degree of legitimacy, since there was an effort to differentiate Hamas as a terrorist organization and as a provider of social services. This legitimacy has increased now that, through the electoral process, Hamas heads the Palestinian Government. It also has the ability to use its educational institutions and youth organizations as a means of recruiting individuals to engage in rock throwing, demonstrations and, among the most committed, suicide bombings and other terrorists operations. Moreover these organizations along with cultural clubs provide a very effective means by which revenues can be raised and hidden so that they can later be employed in conducting terrorists operations while providing cover for those in Hamas who are involved in engaging in attacks.

While there are a number of other leading terrorist groups, the best known of them is Al Qaeda. It is unique for a variety of reasons. In the first place, it is often referred to as a form of entrepreneurial terrorism, since its original leader Osama Bin Laden, born in Saudi Arabia, was the son of a leading businessman and in his own right amassed a personal fortune that continued to grow from his various businesses even after he fully committed himself to his version of Islamic fundamentalism. His deep pockets gave him a level of independence since he was not dependent on state sponsorship. Secondly, while Bin Laden became radicalized when he fought the Mujahideen against the Soviet Occupation in Afghanistan, he ultimately is known for creating a terrorist network which, truly international in scope, has brought together individuals and groups who may share common values in regard to waging their form of Jihad against those who do not subscribe to their beliefs, but who also pursue their own regional agendas, whether it be in Malaysia and Indonesia or France or Germany. It is therefore important to recognize that Al Qaeda is difficult to destroy since it is in effect not a typically organized group, but a movement that, in a very real sense, franchises global terrorism through ideological and tactical guidance. As well, it provides the informal channels which can assist in arming and financing local terrorists groups and individuals who have shown their capability of operating together, whether such operations took place during the first attack on the World Trade Center or the events of 9/11, the American embassy bombings in Kenya and Tanzania in 1988 or the attack on the USS *Cole* in Yemen in 2000. Al Qaeda represents the initiation of a new generation of terrorism: a terrorism that not only is fully international in scope and operations but also is coordinated through the Internet in what – as we shall see in chapter 6 – is what has aptly been identified as "netwar."

This ambitious strategy has been spelled out in a number of publications and fatwas (religious edicts) by Bin Laden and his supporters. In contrast to other groups who provide a general strategy or goals, Al Qaeda has different strategic phases. As one eminent authority notes:

> As defined by Osama, Al Qaeda has short, mid- and long-term strategies. Before 9/11, its immediate goal was the withdrawal of US troops from Saudi Arabia and the creation there of a Caliphate. Its mid-term strategy was the ouster of the "apostate rulers" of the Arabian Peninsula and thereafter the Middle East and the creation of true Islamic states. And the long term strategy was to build a formidable array of Islamic states – including ones with nuclear capability – to wage war on the US (the "Great Satan") and its allies.[8]

Al Qaeda, through its sophisticated network, its ready ability to acquire funds and its overarching religious ideology – which can provide a common basis for joint operations by different groups – remains a major threat to governments constrained by their own political agendas, issues of sovereignty and domestic and international law.

Al Qaeda has also been able to expand its network and its influence through widespread use of the internet. Not only does the organization use it to solicit new members, frequently it is used to broadcast attacks to the wider audience. Images of scores of captives taken hostage in the Iraq war and elsewhere have been broadcast over the world-wide-web as a bargaining chip for the terrorists to wield. Many groups are now adopting this tactic, which can not only expand the number of people any given act is likely to reach, but can also intensify the experience for the viewers of the videos and statements because it is far more personal in nature. Increases in the usage of computers have also made terrorists better able to maintain their anonymity. With this increased security, terrorists can grow bolder both in terms of whom they work with as well as whom they direct their tactics at.

There are of course a variety of other groups ranging from Hezbollah – which has major political and armed forces in Lebanon –

to other groups within the Middle East, South Asia and Northern Africa who are more than willing to work with Al Qaeda. Supporters of these groups have also forged real or imagined marriages of convenience outside of Al Qaeda, directed against what they perceive as secular societies of the West which, they maintain, are led by the United States.

In addition, such traditional territorial-based old-line groups as the Basque Fatherland and Liberty (ETA) are still seeking to secede from Spain and establish their own state in both Spanish and French territory. Also, despite progress the "troubles" in Northern Ireland remain, as both the Provisional Wing of the Irish Republican Army (PIRA) and the Ulster Volunteer Force (UVF) engage in terrorism for their Catholic and Protestant core supporters. There are of course other separatist forces that have used and will use terrorism as a tactic in their own wars of liberation, be they the Tamil Tigers in Sri Lanka or Chechen separatists.

It is also important to recognize that a wide variety of hate and extremist groups remain active in the postindustrialized West as xenophobia over immigration policies continues. Such groups have not been a focus as a result of the concern over international terrorists in the "global war on terrorism," but they have the capabilities to engage in their own form of terrorism. The legacy of the bombing of the Federal Building in Oklahoma remains.

Western religious fundamentalists who resort to violence, ironically, share much in terms of their zealotry with their Middle Eastern counterparts, The Army of God, for example, who engage in terrorism against abortion clinics and their personnel, provide what could be viewed as their own non-Muslim fatwa as seen in the following declaration.

Beginning officially with the passage of the Freedom of Choice Act – we, the remnants of God-fearing men and women of the United States of Amerika, do officially declare war on the entire child-killing industry. After praying, fasting and making continual supplication to God for your pagan, heathen, infidel souls we then peacefully, passively presented our bodies in front of your death camps … No longer: All the options are expired! All options have expired! Our Most Dread Sovereign Lord God requires that whoever sheds man's blood, by man shall his blood be shed.[9]

Finally, there are other special-interest groups who will pursue violence as a strategy to achieve their goals. One of these groups, the Earth Liberation Front (ELF), has been exceedingly active in attacking resorts and other facilities which they believe are contributing to the degradation of the environment. The following communiqué shows their anger, their willingness to use violence in the name of an ideology that takes from both old and new movements who have resorted to terrorism.

We are the burning rage of this dying planet. The war of greed ravages the earth and species die out every day. ELF works to speed up the collapse of industry, to scare the rich and to undermine the state, we embrace social and deep ecology practical resistance movement. We have to show the enemy that we are serious about defending what is sacred. Together we have teeth and claws to match our dreams ... Since 1992, a series of earth nights and Halloween smashes has mushroomed around the world, thousands of bulldozers, power lines, computer systems, buildings and valuable equipment have been composed ... We take inspiration from the Luddites, Levelers, Diggers, the Autonme squatter movement, ALF, The Zapatistas ... and the little people.[10]

There are of course many other terrorists groups varying from large, well-organized groups that have the membership and resources to engage in international operations, to small, single cells that may lack the capability to conduct complex simultaneous multiple attacks. But in the world of terrorism's sophisticated ideologies, strategies and clearly defined goals may not be necessary to generate fear to the largest possible audience. As we well know the action of a lone killer in Sarajevo and a sniper in a book repository in Dallas literally changed history. In terrorism, size does not necessarily matter.

Tactics

It is not the purpose of this section to specifically address the tactics – that is, the operational arts of those who engage in terrorism. To do so is to provide yet another primer that can be used in the conduct of actual operations. Unfortunately there is no limit of what can only be called training manuals ranging from the now very outdated but still lethal directions found in the *Anarchist Cookbook* to a virtual library that ranges from basic to highly sophisticated information on how to conduct any number of different attacks.[11] Nevertheless it is prudent to discuss basic tactical patterns that can assist the reader and his or her family and friends in developing basic measures to help them avoid the danger – however remote – of becoming direct victims of terrorism. Furthermore, time and time again it has become readily apparent that, with the exception of indiscriminate assaults, terrorist will look for what are called "softer" targets of opportunity. It can make a difference if one takes basic and often commonsense precautions. Moreover, an appreciation of the tactics of terrorists reinforces a basic theme of this book – that terrorism is not mindless, but purposeful violence. Therefore, an appreciation of the operational art, however general, can assist us in understanding and not primarily reacting to the next threat or incident.

While there is a current concern over terrorist innovation in tactics and capabilities, especially in the realm of weapons of mass destruction (WMD), the fact remains that terrorists tend to be conservative in tactics and use of explosives and weapons.

The most common terrorist attack remains the bombing, which has been a hallmark of terrorism from the classic anarchist devices in the late nineteenth and early twentieth centuries to a whole new host of explosive materials. Particularly starting in the late 1960s, the weapon of choice was the bomb and the selection was largely based on the following reasons.

First, the bomb was primarily used as a weapon of indiscriminate destruction. This factor created the greatest fear in the public since there was a recognition that anyone could be at the wrong place at the right time. Whether bombing took place in a crowded street in Frankfurt or a railway station in Milan, the basic psychological response of the public was "there but for the grace of God go I." In effect, terrorism was no longer an abstract concept and acts were not directed at specific targets, but at everyone. It became a salient threat to the general public.

Secondly, the bombing was relatively simple to conduct, since if the choice of victims was indiscriminate, so were the targets. The terrorists had an incredible range of locations and facilities in which to launch their attack. Unless they had specific targets in mind, which might be "hardened," they could, in effect, strike anywhere. Consequently, authorities had to cope with the impossible challenge of trying to provide overarching security. The fact was, there were too many targets, too few resources and warnings in too little time to prevent all potential attacks.

Thirdly, bombing enabled terrorists to carry out the attack and then leave, quite possibly to prepare to engage in future assaults. This, of course, would change with the advent of the suicide bombing, but to this day the "conventional" (as contrasted to a suicide) bombing remains the major choice used by terrorists, be it on subway trains in Spain or the use of improvised explosive devices (IEDs) in Iraq.

A second very common terrorist tactic involves hostage taking and kidnapping. The impact of hostage taking was sometimes very politically significant, occasionally involving the captivity and, in a number of cases, the murder of high-profile hostages. The murder of the former Prime Minister of Italy, Aldo Moro, by the Red Brigades, the seizure of General Dozier by the Red Army Faction and the seizure of the OPEC ministers in Vienna by the notorious terrorist Carlos (the Jackal) sent shock waves in both domestic and international politics. Perhaps the most publicized kidnapping, aside from the Munich Massacre – where the perpetrators engaged in an overt public act that challenged authorities to directly respond – was the Iranian hostage crisis.

Hostage taking and kidnapping still remain major forms of terrorism, but with a difference. Increasingly, while the acts may be justified on the basis of a political cause to dramatize and raise revenue for a cause, they are for all intents and purposes nonpolitical criminal acts. Thus, for example, the Abu Sayaf Group that initially engaged in hostage taking as part of a political agenda now has engaged in such actions simply for personal financial gain. Moreover, there is a successful criminal business for ransoms that are paid by corporations and families despite the fact that many countries have laws making such payments illegal.

As in the case of hostage taking, skyjacking became a major tactic of terrorism in the late 1960s and 1970s. The first recorded skyjacking took place over the period February 21 to March 2, 1931 when rebel soldiers in Peru took two US pilots hostage and forced them to drop propaganda leaflets over Lima, an event that would be eerily replicated when Croatian nationalists seized a Trans World Airlines aircraft and forced its crew to drop leaflets over Paris. The resort to skyjacking had a profound impact in the history of modern terrorism. As noted earlier, such actions ushered in the area of non-territorial terrorism, but in addition, they were inherently dramatic and provided the terrorists with a rapidly shifting stage on which to dramatize their causes.

Skyjackings also place great strain on authorities to preempt such actions and are exceedingly difficult to end once they are in progress. Finally the economic cost involved in the loss of business and tourist revenues and the cost incurred to provide effective security measures was enormous. The impact of skyjacking has of course become even more significant with the events of 9/11 as aircraft became man-guided weapons of mass destruction by airborne suicide bombers.

It should also be noted that the conventional weapons of terrorists are still the most lethal despite the new technology of destruction that is available to them. The pistol, the rifle and the assault weapon are readily available, unfortunately and their impact may be profound if one could add up the figures of those murdered by such weapons in terrorist attacks. Also, those who use such weapons can acquire instantaneous media coverage and represent a major challenge to law enforcement – as in the case of the hostage taking in a Moscow theater or the seizure of children at school in Beslan.

Moreover, while they were not acts of terrorism, in school shootings in the United States the use of conventional weapons raises serious questions that are only now being addressed. Finally, it is worth noting how one or two individuals armed with sniper rifles, even without a political agenda, can immobilize the operation of government of a super-power as in the case of the Washington, DC, snipers.

What is especially ominous now is the increased availability of what are called "stand-off weapons" which can enable a terrorist to target a facility, a person or an aircraft at a considerable distance, to inflict major destruction and more than likely evade the authorities. Moreover, as in the case of the indiscriminate bombing where it is impossible for authorities to "harden" all potential targets, there is little that can be done with the medium of aerospace terrorism such as 9/11.

Irrespective of the change, the continuity of terrorism remains and unfortunately will be enhanced – that is, the ability to purposefully use the threat and resort to violence to intimidate a broad audience. The difficulty now is that with the availability of new technologies the terrorists might have the ability not only to intimidate but also to maim and kill the audience.

As mentioned above, with the increased usage of the internet as a tool by terrorists, the audience which they can reach with their violence will grow larger. However, a second, possibly more dangerous, aspect of the increased technology might be worse still. With more and more countries coming online and with access improving in nations all over the world, the terrorists will have thousands more people to influence in terms of ideas. No matter the security of any nation, terrorists can now find a way to recruit, using their rhetoric to establish wings or cells in countries worldwide. The problem is exacerbated by the problem of the youth, often disaffected themselves, being those with the best access to and knowledge of emerging technology.

Preparing for the Attack and the Implications for Personal and Family Responsibilities in Addressing the Threat

An understanding of the basic tactics of terrorism can help individuals and families lessen their chance of being a target. It must be noted that there are no fail-safe solutions, but the likelihood of a physical attack leading to death is far more remote than death while driving. Nevertheless, especially in troubled areas, forms of self-help antiterrorism measures have a role to play.

At the outset, it must be noted that even in smaller terrorists cells and groups there is a need to engage in the organizational stage if one is to ultimately engage in operations. At this phase the challenge of identifying and apprehending potential terrorists largely falls under the purview of the authorities with the key role of national security and police intelligence to identify and apprehend potential terrorists before they are at the stage of preparing for the conduct of operations. This is a daunting task for even the most professional organizations, given the precautions taken by terrorists from their secret bases of operations whether in a rural area or the urban jungle. The extent of the care taken to not compromise security in an urban environment can be readily seen in the Al Qaeda manual section entitled "Security Precautions Related to Apartments." The guidance is quite specific:

(1) Choosing the apartment carefully as far as location. The size for the work necessary (meetings, storage, arms. fugitives, work preparation).
(2) It is preferable to rent apartments on the ground floor to facilitate escape and digging of trenches.
(3) Preparing secret locations in the apartment for securing document, records, arms and other important items.

(4) Preparing ways of vacating the apartment in case of a surprise attack (stands, wooden ladders).[13]

The ability to identify and apprehend terrorists in this phase calls for a high degree of what is called "trade craft" in intelligence. But the public can assist, especially after the terrorists' organizational phase has been completed and preparation for the operation takes place. At this time the terrorists enter the surveillance stage and it is at this crucial stage where they must leave the security of their clandestine cells, begin to prepare actively for their assault and select targets by engaging in attack reconnaissance. It is here where an individual, his or her family and friends or a neighborhood can play the important role of engaging in the crime-watch measures already practiced in many communities to identify suspicious behavior and report it to the appropriate authorities.

In the final analysis, what is the difference between reporting to the authorities a strange car whose passengers may be preparing either a robbery or a terrorist bombing? Moreover, what is the difference between the reporting of a strange smell from a house, where the inhabitants may on one hand have a methamphetamine drug laboratory or on the other a bomb factory (in both of which the dangers of explosion are very real)? Admittedly, care must be taken to avoid promoting paranoia and engaging in dangerous stereotyping of individuals as a means of identifying potential terrorists, but one can and should differentiate between an individual's appearance and his or her actions.

The assassination of Spanish Prime Minister Luis Carrero Blanco on December 20, 1973, by Basque separatists of the Euskadi Ta Askatasuna (ETA), is a good illustration of the failure of basic crime-watch techniques. In that case the Minister, devoutly Roman Catholic, went to mass at the same time each day. Knowing this, the perpetrators tunneled under a major street in Madrid across from the church, over a number of weeks and on the appointed day they detonated a mine that was so powerful that Blanco's car – now in the Military Museum near the Prado – went over a four-storey building and over an overhang before it landed on a roof. Had someone had the curiosity to ask what these individuals were doing, perhaps the attack could have been prevented. Unfortunately, in too many instances, people report suspicious behavior only after the act has occurred. Crime watch in general and in regard to terrorism specifically, cannot be effective if an individual provides information with the useless benefit of hindsight after an attack.

The risk of apprehension for the terrorists is likely if there is appropriate public awareness during the next stage of preparation for a terrorist incident, the rehearsal stage. Many incidents do not have a "run through," but in complex operations it can be anticipated that the terrorists will have a drill despite the dangers to themselves. The problem is that while the risk of identification and capture increases during this period, their time is running out and the attack will shortly take place: the terrorists fear failure more than capture in many cases.

The final stages of movement to the target, execution and getaway will be in the investigative hands of the police and security forces. While public input can be important in tracking down the terrorists after an attack, the damage has already been done.

What to Do if the Threat Becomes a Reality

There are a wide variety of books and manuals that address what families and victims should do if the unthinkable happens and they are subject to a terrorism attack. They cover such issues as personal security measures and individual and corporate crisis management, as well as issues associated with kidnap and ransom insurance, how an individual should behave in captivity, how the family should cope with the crisis and a whole range of other considerations. There are, however, some basic security measures which can be quickly presented and can make a difference in the event of an incident.

To start with, it is important that the family, as a security unit, discusses whether there is a threat to them and, if so, how they should deal with that threat. This would most readily apply in situations when the family or one of its members goes to work in a high-threat environment. Some basic considerations include whom to contact and what necessary personal information should be kept on file for the authorities in the event of a crisis. For example, on a normal day does one know the color of his or her significant other's eyes much less his or her blood type and medical requirements? So how about on a day where a family member is injured or abducted in an attack? The key is to discuss concerns frankly, including with the youngsters, in such a way that awareness takes place without creating paranoia. It is worth recalling that it is what we don't know that generates and intensifies fear.

Furthermore, if appropriate measures are taken, the family of the victim will have a basis from which to act and at the same time the victim, as a hostage for example, will at least know that he or she has effectively prepared with the family to deal with a crisis. The uncertainty of captivity need not be compounded by the guilt of not having a family security plan in place.

If there is an indiscriminate bombing it is vital that individuals move away from the blast area for the following reasons.

- First, unless volunteer help is required, well-intentioned but ill-trained citizens can act as an impediment for the police and rescue units.
- Second and perhaps most ominous, is the fact that terrorists often set off two detonations, one to kill and maim the victims and a second to do the same to the units coming to their aid. Unnecessary curiosity can kill.
- Third, there is now a troublesome change in the conventional wisdom concerning hostage taking. In the past, emphasis was placed on the victim not fighting back at the start of an incident, based on the assumption that any quick action might lead to a disastrous result by a terrorist who is in a combat mode during the uncertain, very hectic early phases of an operation. Moreover, it was viewed to be a valid edict that time was on the side of the authorities. The security forces and negotiators outside a barricaded area could increasingly

control the environment and use it for leverage against the hostage taker. Unfortunately, these assumptions are now very much open to question, as today's terrorists may have no desire to negotiate, especially when they are in a suicide operation; the fact that there are governments who will be either unable or unwilling to combat the terrorists – and thus indirectly support their goals – adds to this questioning. The stakes are now higher and, increasingly, a potential victim will have to make the literally life-or-death decision of whether it is advisable to attempt an escape.

Finally, there are a wide variety of coping techniques that apply to both the victim and their family.

Taking the Initiative

There is now recognition that terrorism is not what happens to the other person in another place. The insularity and false sense of security, especially in the United States, was shattered with the bombing at the Federal Building in Oklahoma City and the events of 9/11. But despite this new awareness, the fact remains that individuals, families, neighborhoods, states and nations often tend to let down their guard after the intense activity that follows each terrorist incident. That being said, at all levels it is vital that we avoid the danger of going from under- to overreaction after the next major attack. Ultimately, just as terrorists have effectively achieved a unity of effort acting locally through their own networks as well as in the international arena, how communities respond to the reality is just as important because, as noted before, all terrorism is ultimately local. To act means to not simply return to indifference and normalcy and expect the government to provide a blanket of security. The techniques of counterterrorism crime watch can be applied as an early-warning system and a frontline in the defense against terrorism.

In the final analysis, terrorism is directed at all of us and we all have the responsibility individually and collectively to meet the challenge within the limits of the law. Moreover, the challenge should not be met through the use of stereotyping and other measures targeting individuals who, because of their religious or ethnic background, can become scapegoats. To do this is not only to engage in an indirect form of terrorism, but to spread the hatred that feeds the appetite of those who practice terrorism.

–5–

The Attack and its Enduring Legacy

The Psychological Impact of Terrorism

After an incident of terrorism, it is the psychological damage that has the greatest impact on those who have been directly involved as well as on those who, through the media, have witnessed the violence. It is the "shelf life" of the impact that has a profound effect on the individual, the community and the political and social order. It is worth repeating the adage that terrorism is aimed at the people watching. Those who resort to terrorism are ultimately conducting a form of psychological warfare that may have significant political consequences. In this chapter individual behavior as related to hostage taking will be addressed, as will the broader impact on the community resulting from bombings and other incidents of greater magnitude.

On the individual level, people of course react differently to the violence they have witnessed. A great deal of research has focused on hostage behavior, because it is an ongoing process (as contrasted to the finality of a bombing) to the immediate victim and because hostage taking was a major form of terrorist attack in the 1970s and 1980s as part of a political agenda and is now increasingly motivated for criminal profit.

There have been a number of excellent books and articles on how one should attempt to cope with seizure and captivity. Most address how an individual will or should attempt to behave at the moment of capture and then provide coping skills which may help an individual or group to endure and survive imprisonment. It is worth knowing the basics, since – as noted before – it is what we don't understand that amplifies our fear. Also, that lack of knowledge can impact how a family will adjust when a member is seized, especially since the family itself is thus also being emotionally held hostage.

At the outset it should be noted that being held hostage is, in a number of ways, more difficult than being a prisoner of war (POW) or a convict. In both of those cases there are specific expectations of the roles and rules that must be followed. In the former instance, the POW has a code of conduct that will ideally help to guide his or her behavior. If they adhere to the rules of the most senior prisoners available and those who captured them, such prisoners are protected from excesses in varying degrees by the Geneva Convention rules of protection of POWs. Even in a jail or penitentiary there are specific regulations that must be followed. The dangers of inmate-to-inmate violence is, of course, ever present, but the rules that are laid down by the authority give some degree of predictability in terms of length of sentence and whether one can get time off for good behavior. In contrast, not only is a hostage faced with a life-threatening situation, but also may experience a degree of normlessness, since there may not be a specific role or duties that he or she is expected to follow, much less being trained for. Moreover, unlike the convict in particular, there is no clear sentence. The hostage may be summarily executed in days or be involved in a captivity lasting years. Therefore it is important that hostages attempt to replace the profound uncertainty created by the "normlessness" of their incarceration and attempt to define their role and accompanying behavior.

In addressing the means of adjustment, the work of Douglas Derrer *We Are All Targets*, provides excellent and concise guidance on behavior.[1] Derrer is a psychologist and officer in the US Navy who has been involved in training military personnel to deal with captivity and his insights are quite relevant to civilians who are potential hostages. He presents six stages of becoming a prisoner or hostage and suggests coping measures. As we shall note, a number of these measures may also be of help to the family and a broader community.

Stage One: Startle/Panic – Seconds to Minutes.   This takes place at the initial seizure. The victim is confused, disoriented and quite possibly in a state of panic. This is an exceedingly dangerous time for the victim since he or she may experience a fight-or-flight reaction. The danger is comparable to the behavior of the captors, who in their own right – irrespective of their degree of training – are in a combat mode and therefore capable of reacting or overreacting to any attempt by the victim to flee. It is therefore important for the victim to attempt to not engage in a panic reaction and to follow the orders of the captors, since any overreaction can lead to a fatal conclusion.

There are, however, two words of cautions to be noted here. First of all, increasingly there are groups who do not wish to take hostages. In such an extreme position their potential victim may have to make a very dangerous judgment call and fight back.

Secondly, a word of warning about self-defense measures is in order. A well-trained individual who, possessing martial arts skills, can react quickly and negate the impact of panic may indeed affect his or her escape. But, an individual with rudimentary training may put him- or herself in jeopardy. There is quite a difference between flipping an instructor in a gym and attempting to do the same with a well-armed determined adversary. In each case, both in terrorism and in regard to ordinary crime ranging from purse-snatching to armed assault, one must ask if its is worth fighting for the loss of property that can be replaced as contrasted to loss of a life.

Stage Two: Disbelief – Minutes to Hours.   This has implications for both the immediate victim and the family. It is normal for individuals who experience a loss to be psychologically numbed and engage in a form of denial. But as long as denial takes place, it will be harder for both the victim and the family to engage in the difficult task of adjusting to trauma of hostage-taking and other forms of violence and terrorism. Even in a broader sense, governments and countries have suffered a form of collective denial in regard to the threat of terrorism by maintaining that "It can't happen here."

Or it's "an isolated incident." To accept a reality is to begin to adjust to it.

Stage Three: Hyper-vigilance – Hours to Days. This is particularly significant for captives, as it is a stage where the initial shock and numbness is replaced by an attention to detail and the beginning of knowledge of the ones surrounding them and the circumstances of their captivity. By doing so, victims begin not only to understand but to have some control over the new environment.

Stage Four: Resistance and Compliance. This requires an individual to address the delicate balance of not being viewed as simply a compliant victim without an individual identity on one hand, while on the other avoiding the danger of antagonizing the captor to the degree that the victim's actions can lead to injury or death. The need for the victim to assert him- or herself in part calls for establishing a routine, engaging in exercise as a means of seeking some degree of control over the environment and keeping in mind that others are seeking his or her release. "Keeping the faith can help individuals survive the long night."[2] Also, mental activities ranging from building a house in one's mind to revisiting places one enjoyed in the past have been used to keep active in the confines of a prison.

Stage Five: Depression – Weeks to Months. This is a most difficult time for the captive when, as Derrer notes, many experience "hitting the bottom." It is important during this period to keep mentally active and, if the captive is not alone, to communicate with his fellow prisoners for mental support.

Stage Six: Gradual Acceptance – Months to Years. This is, of course, difficult to conceive of, yet it has worked and is a testimony to individuals' strength and will to survive. On a personal level, I had the pleasure of knowing an individual who was held in solitary confinement, after his aircraft was shot down in Vietnam, for more than six years. He mentioned that after the first day he never felt in solitary because he was able to communicate with his fellow prisoners by tapping codes on the walls. But perhaps even more significant were his comments about the duration of his stay; as he said, "I took one day at a time."[3]

His advice should also be considered by the captive's family. There will be ups and downs, but if one rides the emotional roller coaster, such an experience might lead to a deeper depression. It is important to maintain a degree of equilibrium, keep the faith and seek to maintain a routine while fighting for the release of a loved one.

Clearly there is now recognition that it is imperative for anyone who has been directly subject to a terrorist attack, be it a bombing or a kidnapping, to seek counseling as soon as possible. The longer the delay the more difficult it will be for the individual and his or her family to adjust to the often primal fears that are the tragic products of terrorism.

Until the hostage-takings in the 1970s and early 1980s the need for psychological intervention was often ignored. In part, this form of denial was based on the fact that individuals might feel that they were somehow weak if they sought counseling. This is especially true among first responders who initially failed to recognize that they were impacted upon almost as much as the victims they sought to rescue. It is therefore vital that individuals, despite their assessments of their own perceived inward strength, recognize that no one walks away without some level of psychological harm after an attack. If one keeps in mind that highly motivated and trained professional military personnel and their superiors ultimately recognized the need for intervention after captivity and torture, there should be an acceptance of the vital need by the general population for psychological as well as medical support and guidance. It is not the purpose of this chapter to address the coping mechanisms that are available – that should be left to the mental health professionals – but it is vital to note that the immediate victims, even if they are not physically injured, do not just "psychologically walk away" from the profoundly disturbing experience they went through.

Coping as a Community with Acts of Terrorism: The Immediate Cost

Most of us, of course, will not be directly impacted by terrorists' acts as the result of captivity, injury or death of family or friends, but we all have been impacted upon by terrorism. The word "impacted" is intentionally used instead of "victimized." If we permanently take on the role of victims, we run the risk of reacting to past and future incidents essentially by wearing a mantle of fear instead of effectively coping with a threat that most certainly will continue into the coming years. How communities – be they towns, cities, states or countries – adjust to the next attack will have serious implications on whether the terrorists will continue to use fear as a means to influence our lives and direct our behavior and – if those communities respond incorrectly – could effectively make governments pursue the wrong policies in combating terrorism. Terrorism is ultimately an antisocial act that seeks to destroy the fabric of the social and political order by forcing people to give in as a group to fear, despair, helplessness and rage.

The full impact of concerted campaigns or singular major acts of terrorism are difficult to assess since they can have a very broad and diverse effect on a targeted area, be it physical loss of life and injuries, damage to the critical infrastructure of a community or its financial well being. Moreover, while there is extensive experience in regard to dealing with natural disasters, there is a degree of acceptance of such events since they are not the deliberate result of a purposeful activity perpetrated by man. Even if the disaster is caused by human error and technological failure, because it was not a deliberate act there is not the fear that the perpetrators might cause it again.

Also adding to the impact of a terrorist attack, while there has been much experience with natural disasters, there has been significantly less experience of the results in regard to a terrorist attack. The refinement of emergency and crisis-management techniques for dealing with such tragedies as flood, tornados, tidal waves, chemical spills, air crashes and a whole host of other natural and man-created disasters, doesn't necessarily prepare those first responders or the communities they serve, for the impact of a terrorist event. Now, especially with the profound impact of the events of 9/11 and the London and Madrid bombings, with the willingness and capability of terrorists to engage in mass terrorism, communities must recognize that we all must cope with intentional disasters that may be part of a campaign of terrorism. This coping must include not only the short-term physical costs in life and property, but must also deal with the long-term psychological, financial and communication problems that result from the attack no matter the preparation of the community.

This may be especially true in the case of repeated attacks such as the London bombings. While a single attack can shock a nation and the world, repeated attacks of the same nature truly shake the foundation of society. Because people operate, in general, with the idea that their world is safe for them to live in, multiple attacks remove that illusion and, for many, can make it difficult to function at a normal level.

The impact on the community has parallels with the impact of the act on the individual immediate victims. One must of course be careful to not neatly equate individual with collective behavior, but the individual person's shock, disorientation, acceptance and having to come to terms with an act of terrorism also applies to the community. Tragically, how a community adjusts is only presently being fully studied, now that we are increasingly experiencing the age of mass terrorism. As noted earlier, that adjustment will help to determine whether the terrorists have or have not achieved their goal of intimidation of the largest audience possible.

One cannot downplay the potential impact on the community. To a small community, the death of three may send emotional shock-waves which, for all intents and purposes, are comparable to a form of mass psychological terrorism. But the scope of the impact in large-scale incidents serves to underscore the reality that the number of people who have to adjust after any incident goes beyond the hundreds or thousands. While the full effect, especially in the long term, of the psychological impact has yet to be determined, various figures show that a large community, even if it is not directly traumatized by an attack, is indirectly affected.

Thus, in the Oklahoma City bombing, the most destructive terrorist attack in the United States at the time, in which 168 died, 853 were injured, thirty children were orphaned and 219 more lost one of their parents, there was a profound emotional rippling effect. That is, when one moves beyond the relatively easy physical damage assessments which included nine structures suffering full or partial collapse, twenty others demolished and 800 buildings receiving damage, which in itself is of great magnitude, the physical damage pales in comparison to the mental fallout which one might add is, in the case of Oklahoma City, small compared to the destruction of 9/11. Consider that in Oklahoma City, 16,744 people worked or resided in the area where the bomb impacted and 80 percent of the schools within the Oklahoma City School District had children with immediate family members who were killed or injured. When one also notes that out of a city population of nearly 500,000, more than 38,000 people knew someone who was killed or injured and an estimated 190,000 people went to funerals, one can readily appreciate how one bomb can be, as noted earlier, a profound fear and psychological "force multiplier."[4]

Given these grim figures on the real and perceived involvement of the public in this incident, what can one say about the magnitude of the sarin gas attack in Tokyo, 9/11 aircraft suicide bombings in New York and Washington, the subway bombings in London and the next large urban attack?

Coping as a Community: The Long-term Challenge of Adjustment

When one considers the profound and personal impact on a community resulting from a terrorist attack, it is understandable that one wonders how a community – be it a town, city or in a broader sense, nation – can make an adjustment back to relative normalcy after an attack. The phrase "relative normalcy" is used for two reasons. In the first place, it is by no means clear what constitutes normalcy, especially in a large urban area where change and accompanied conflicts can often be viewed to be the rule and not the exception. Secondly, whether one is referring to an individual or collective response to a major terrorist act, despite the common use of the term, there is no closure to an incident. The human and psychological cost may change, but the legacy remains. One should therefore not talk of some idealized final "closure." Nevertheless, a community can and should seek to make an adjustment to post-terrorist incident trauma. In order to achieve this goal it is important at the outset to recognize that communities are far more than geographical locations or legalistic-political entities. Depending on many factors they may contract or expand, stagnate or remain vital, for ultimately the community is an organic construct that, to varying degrees, people identify with or participate in. On any normal day individuals may, through their social associations, identify with people in the neighborhood, whereas in a time of large natural or man-made disaster, the sense of community may expand outward to a city, a state and, indeed, even a nation. Guessing how long a sense of community will remain after a disaster is problematic, but one can suggest that after a major event the sense of community will contract to a sense of place far smaller than the nation-state. Communities are not only subject to change, they may also be flexible and permeable – flexible in terms of adjusting to new conditions and permeable, being capable of allowing for and absorbing outside change.

The ability or inability of a community to adjust after an attack varies greatly given the circumstances of the attack, the community's size, ethnic make-up, income level, location and a myriad of other factors. But a positive adjustment can be made to help a community recover from the shock of a terrorist act in the following manners. In the first place, very much as in an individual adjustment to a trauma, the community will seek to readjust after the event has happened. In the short term and – this is quite positive – there may be an assertion of community consciousness and cooperation as individuals in all walks of life may share the same concerns and achieve a degree of mutual cooperation. Certainly this awareness and cooperation could be readily seen in such events as the Oklahoma City Bombing, in the events of 9/11 and on other occasions where people collectively rose to the challenge. But it must also be recognized that the line between cooperation and conflict is a thin one and in some environments the impact of an incident, the rumor mill, the existence of deep seated ethnic or religious animosities, can lead to disorder and civil strife. Nevertheless, communities at large have often shown their best faces while physically, psychologically and socially dealing with a critical situation.

The ability to develop a sense of community after an incident cannot be force-fed through the use of crisis-management plans or emergent management techniques. The key to developing a sense of community to deal with critical situations and increasingly with the challenges created by the threat of mass terrorism, is the forging of interpersonal and accompanying interorganizational relations which can assist in creating a community bond *before* a crisis. This requires a combination of skillful identification of community leadership and organizations that can step in to assist the authorities if a disaster takes place. To achieve the goal of community bonding is of course no easy task, but it is well worth spending the time to do so if a combination of community involvement and education can strengthen ties that will hold and indeed be reinforced *during* and *after* a large-scale emergency. As noted earlier, the concept of terrorism awareness – crime watch with muscle – not only enables individuals to be informed about potential threats and how to identify, report and deal with them, but more importantly makes them participants, stakeholders, in protecting their community even more than they already were.

In meeting what is unfortunately an enduring and growing danger, an informed public discussion at the neighborhood level, in town hall or through various social and religious organizations can forge the bonds that will make a difference during and after an act of terrorism. Participation is the key.[5]

How a community will respond in both the short and the long term will also be dependent on the availability of and willingness of individuals and families not only to seek medical and financial support after a crisis but to recognize a need for and access to mental-health professionals who can provide the counseling that will continue long after the first responders have left, governmental services have been reconstituted and there is more or less a return to normalcy. The availability of counseling that should be in place *before* a crisis cannot fully fall under the purview of governmental services. It is absolutely essential that a wide variety of voluntary, charitable and nongovernmental organizations be actively involved in planning any disaster and postdisaster mental-health support. Moreover, it is also vital that planners determine which organizations are both reputable and able to carry out their functions. Unfortunately, after terrorist incidents there still are too many outwardly charitable private organizations that seek to manipulate the feelings of individuals for profit. Excellent support for advice in regard to identifying appropriate organizations and developing community plans are readily available in the United States through the officers of the Department of Homeland Security, the Federal Emergency Management Agency (FEMA) and others. In addition, the vast experience of the Red Cross, the Salvation Army and other such organizations provides a wealth of information on the topic of planning for and execution of disaster management, which should be drawn upon.

There is one area of concern often not directly dealt with after a major tragedy, a problem associated with "preserving memory" – that is, how a community recognizes and memorializes victims of terrorism without creating a process that leads to divisions instead of healing a community or how the community promotes an environment to encourage moving on instead of continuing a sense of victimization.[6] It is an especially major challenge to memorialize without victimizing a community. In the first case, whatever the extent of the tragedy, the process of memorializing should not be left solely in governmental or private hands. It should include the community and a spirit of "inclusiveness" that will have not only the victims, the survivors and the families involved, but also the community at large. This is no easy task, especially as the collective emotional scars have not yet begun to heal, but the issue of participation cannot be downplayed. No one has a monopoly on officially recognized grief.

At the risk of being too optimistic, while terrorism is the manifestation of the worst in individuals and groups and its impact on the community can result in great individual and collective physical, psychological and financial cost, events have shown that communities can be and have been brought together in the crucible of a terrorist act. Clearly the impact of that bringing together may not have the same impact as the years progress, but there can be a positive legacy to the tragedy. For, if a community remembers and preserves its history, takes pride in how it worked together, there may be a bond that can transcend one generation. Terrorism can bring out the best and worst in individuals and communities.

Conclusion

Ultimately there will never be a step-by-step solution to how a community can best respond to and cope with acts of terrorism, whether it is a single casualty in a small town or thousands in a large urban area. The pain for both, in part, will be a matter of scale, but the emotional intensity may not differ in either case. The tragedy of a school shooting, for example, is as enduring and searing for the communities involved as is the tragedy for the communities immediately affected by 9/11, the Madrid bombing and other unfortunately notable incidents. In the end, however, the strengths and weaknesses of a community are defined by the people living there. If there is community involvement before an act of terrorism, irrespective of the initial shock, the ability of that community to respond will be heightened. This is as it must be as we enter a changing threat environment to be addressed in the following chapter.

–6–

The Policy Dimensions

On the Community, National
and International Levels

In the final analysis, while the appropriate actions to meet the psychological impact of threats from acts of terrorism – at all levels, ranging from the community to the nation state and beyond – are essential, the fact is that ultimately the political leadership and policy-makers have the responsibility to provide the guidance, legislation and appropriate measures to combat terrorism. Certainly the United States is an example of the complexities faced by the leadership.

The greatest change in the reorganization of those bodies involved in protecting the country from both external and internal threats since the National Security Act of 1947 – which established the Department of Defense and the Central Intelligence Agency – is still very much a work in progress.[1] The creation of the Department of Homeland Security is fundamentally altering the role of US domestic law-enforcement and other agencies in combating terrorism: the Federal Bureau of Investigation is taking on both a domestic and a foreign counterterrorism role in sharp contrast to its traditional functions as the preeminent United States national law-enforcement entity. Moreover, the US military increasingly finds itself involved in the protection of domestic security as contrasted to the defense against external threats. In addition, local police are increasingly being heavily armed much in the tradition of the European Gendarmerie or Guardia Civil. At the same time, the reorganization of American intelligence – with the establishment of a single Director of National Intelligence – is generating great tensions within organizations which seek to preserve their bureaucratic identity and power.[2] The reorganization has also raised the issue as to whether the United States should have its own domestic intelligence organization, modeled after the British MI5.

The problem of reorganizing to meet the changing face of terrorism is of course also keenly felt regionally and internationally as nation-states face the daunting demands to engage in meaningful exchange of information and operational capabilities in the face of an ongoing and increasingly dangerous threat. The task will not be easy, as illustrated by the barriers that must be confronted – not only by the United States but also by other governments – to a new threat environment. Thus an insightful remark, made in *The 9/11 Investigation: Staff Report on the 9/11 Commission* for American political leaders and policy-makers, throws down the gauntlet to those in any nation that has the responsibility of countering terrorism:

> The most difficult thing to get a bureaucracy or a political leader in any system to do after something goes terribly wrong is to acknowledge responsibility for failure. The natural bureaucratic response is to be defensive. Officials hide behind the veil of secrecy or national security or executive privilege. They fear embarrassment, personal and institutional. Elected officials fear retribution from the electorate. Yet demanding accountability from the elected and appointed officials of the government and insisting on revealing and correcting their short comings, are the most basic rights and duties of citizens in a democracy.[3]

By no means are the other implications of the *9/11 Commission Report* limited to the United States. With British MI5 finding it difficult to stop international terror attacks within the UK as the United States did with 9/11, the need for overcoming all types of obstacles becomes clear. Currently MI5 dedicates 44 percent of its resources to international terrorism and an additional 23 percent to domestic security concerns (though this second percentage will likely shrink due to the disarmament of the IRA). With such a high percentage of resources dedicated to stopping attacks, not only at home but internationally, it is certain that counterterrorism efforts by the UK are closely monitored by the government. With the failure to stop the London bombings, many of the same difficult questions that were asked in 9/11 will be asked of those in charge of oversight in the UK.

There is little doubt that more self-assessment of counterterrorism efforts needs to occur in agencies worldwide. Increasingly, nations that have had historical terrorist problems are stepping in to assist with the capture of terrorists. This is a positive development. But with the increased assistance comes the added difficulty of coordination and yet another level of oversight.

At the highest levels of political and bureaucratic leadership, it is therefore vital that the policy-makers accept the reality that it can no longer be business as usual where inertia can continue to act as an impediment to necessary change. Moreover, even if the leadership is in a country that has not experienced major acts of terrorism, it is essential that they go beyond a reactive mode and take, to the best of their ability, the necessary measures to prevent or at least deter or lessen the occurrence or impact of future incidents. To this end, the role of the public in insisting on revealing and correcting their shortcomings is absolutely essential. Appropriate lobbying at all levels is imperative, for it is both a duty and a birthright of the public. Since the risk of terrorism is literally a threat to the general public, that public should exercise its right and insist that political leaders, policy-makers and senior leaders in the bureaucracy move beyond gradual instrumentalism and then overreaction in terms of legislation, funding and training after a particularly destructive incident. To this end, it can be suggested that the following messages should be conveyed to and also initiated by the leadership in meeting the present and future challenges created by terrorism.

First, it must be recognized that the threat of terrorism has been magnified by the public's lack of understanding its context, tactics and strategies for far too long. The intention of this book has been to provide a basis for understanding the framework of a form of violence that is of ancient lineage, but is a contemporary fact of life. But that is only a start.

It is here where education plays such a crucial role. It will only be successful when an understanding of the nature of terrorism is incorporated into the curriculums of both public and private schools ranging from elementary and secondary to colleges and universities.[4] As must be recognized, *how* the nature of terrorism will be addressed, especially among young children, is going to be demanding in order to not intimidate anyone. But we also know that children are like sponges and can uncritically absorb both the words and images portrayed by the mass media after each new outrage. Nor are children immune to listening to and sensing the concern of their parents when the parents are discussing general personal security and crime or if they should consider going on vacation in a country or region that is subject to acts and campaigns of terrorism.

It is always worth repeating that a lack of knowledge, the impact of the image without context and the emotion that is created has unfortunately played into the hands of the terrorists. It is literally what we don't know that gives rise to the generalized fear now pervading societies which finally recognize that terrorism is not what happens to the other person in other countries. Whether it be a history class on the elementary school level or a high school civics class, terrorism should not be viewed as a problem area that somehow does not fit in the mainstream of a curriculum. It is a fact of the human condition and our daily existence and should be treated as such. Admittedly, the developing of what can be called "terrorism understanding" cannot eliminate the initial shock that accompanies any act of terrorism, but it can lessen its impact. As in the case of countering terrorism, it is better to take the educational initiative instead of reacting after the fact where the damage has already been done.

The development of this understanding will create a real – and excellent – opportunity for well-schooled teachers, especially at the secondary school and college and university levels, to address terrorism as an aspect of a classic challenge to democratic ideals, values and processes – namely, the classic task of reconciling civil liberties with the requirements for the protection of individual and minority rights. The need for the reconciliation of these often contradictory fundamental functions of democratic government is perhaps no better illustrated than in the topic of how a democratic political and social order will deal with the next terrorist act. There are excellent books and articles, very effectively addressing the democratic irony of balancing rights and security, that provide a basis for both parents and teachers to address the dilemma. One such classic book is Paul Wilkinson's *Terrorism and the Liberal State*.[5]

A discussion of terrorism also opens doors for an understanding of the need for tolerance and the dangers of prejudice which are the product of many factors. It is no good to simply call for a plea of understanding *after* an attack when innocent people are being persecuted and imprisoned because of the desire for a public to have a scapegoat. An understanding of the values implicit in respecting others' secular and religious values is best taught *before* an incident and not as a form of remediation and educational damage-control after it. An understanding of the principles of Islam by students before the rise of terrorism by fundamentalists who have engaged in an incorrect interpretation of the major precepts of the great religion, to justify the carnage they have inflicted, would have lessened the tensions we now face in increasingly polarized communities. As well, an understanding that *all* the mainstream religions have sometimes justified terrorism in the pursuit of their goals would help to lessen the gap between people with deeply held beliefs and to lessen the self-righteousness that has been used on all sides in the overreaction to terrorist violence. Parents and the community should insist that leaders in public education and the political leadership provide the funding to address terrorism not only to understand it, but also to illustrate what the dangers of intolerance and prejudice can lead to.

Second, it is absolutely vital that the public and the political leadership recognize that terrorism is not simply a series of tragic but essentially episodic events that can be responded to. It is unfortunately true that terrorism not only has been with us for a long period of time but is a protracted form of violence, conflict and warfare – call it what you will – that will continue to threaten our personal, local, national and international security in the years to come.

There will be a requirement for the enunciation at all levels of policies, strategies and operational capabilities that are yet to be fully refined in the battle with a very determined and innovative adversary. While the requirements are complex and beyond the scope of this book, a number of the core attributes in combating terrorism can be enunciated and used as a basis of discussion for those who want not only to understand the enduring threat but to be involved in meeting it.

With the recognition that terrorism is protracted in nature, it is concomitantly important for the authorities to come to terms with the fact that terrorism as a psychological weapon is ultimately a test of will and resolve. As noted earlier, the terrorists, particularly those who believe that both history and religion are on their side, will continue to probe for the weakness in their adversaries and when possible inflict ever more powerful attacks. In response, the immediate victims, their families, the communities, the public at large and the governments involved must recognize that there are no clearly defined strategic victories in an undeclared but global non-territorial form of warfare. All of them face a psychological warfare of attrition where patience, dedication and will determine the outcome of a long-term struggle. This does not mean to imply that there have not been and will not be major successes against terrorists, but we are dealing with an adversary with the dedication and innovation to continually "bring the war home" to their perceived enemies with implacable determination. Our resolve will be tested from one administration to another, from one decade to another. Through education and action the ability of individuals to have faith in their government, largely based on the determination of governments to pursue, capture and eliminate those who engage in terrorism, can create the type of will necessary in fighting what at times appears to be not only a war against all, but a war without end. There may never be total victory, but in the long term, within limits, terrorism can not only be contained, but have its impact diminished.

In the pursuit of this objective, it is absolutely essential that the parochialism created by sovereignty, national interests and arbitrary legalistic boundaries give way to a truly international campaign to counter terrorism. Just as there will never be a universally accepted definition of terrorism, it must also be recognized that there will never be full acceptance of the policies and means to combat terrorism by an often fragmented international community. Yet it should also be noted that even without a universal *definition*, the major *characteristics* of the nature of terrorism have been incorporated into treaties and conventions which have sought to achieve some degree of both condemnation of and cooperation against terrorists and those who sponsor them. Moreover when one moves beyond the heated rhetoric created by different interpretations of approaches to terrorism, there is a level of cooperation not covered in the media (which tend to focus on disunity instead of a meaningful unity) in combating terrorism on the regional and international level. Democratic governments, despite their disagreements, do not want to see their citizens caught unintentionally or intentionally in the cross fire of acts of terrorism. Even authoritarian governments who practice their own forms of state terrorism – terrorism from above – recognize that "terrorism from below" – or agitational terrorism – can not only threaten the stability needed to continue their coercive control, but perhaps, far more significantly, threaten the regime. In many instances these regimes provide financial, logistical and operational support to terrorists groups as long as they don't engage in operations in the state sponsor's own territory.

It is heartening to see especially on the operational level how countries with different interests, ideologies and governments will work together, whether it is to protect their citizens or to eliminate the impact which acts and campaigns of terrorism can have on their national economic well-being in such sensitive areas as the tourist industry. In many cases, given the often secret nature of counterterrorist intelligence and operations against any equally clandestine adversary, countries will not reveal their successes, for such revelations can compromise the "sources and methods" used to identify and capture or eliminate terrorists. Such revelations can also be politically embarrassing to countries who don't wish that their cooperation with particular governments become part of the public record. Perhaps even more ironic is the fact that the success of counterterrorist operations may in part only be assessed by showing that incidents did not happen. But how does one validate that which is not outwardly measurable without revealing the understandably clandestine techniques and cooperation that leads to a success in preventing or responding to terrorism?

While it is important to reemphasize that terrorism is a form of protracted conflict, it should also be noted that anti- and counterterrorism measures have become increasingly effective since the early days of modern terrorism when governments did not fully understand terrorists, much less have the knowledge and assets to combat them. In the antiterrorism arena, the level of technological sophistication to collect and interpret information through "expert systems" and "artificial intelligence" is enhancing the ability of collectors and analysts of terrorism in the public, corporate and academic sectors to identify and develop courses of action to meet the challenges to security caused by terrorism. Moreover, the proliferation of sophisticated technologies to harden targets has gone far beyond the traditional gates and keys that were associated with physical security measures.

But, as noted earlier, there is a cost to these technological advances. The dangers of increasingly witnessing the emergence of a "surveillance society" should not be dismissed. The classic problem of reconciling public security and one's private zone will continue and in all probability will become even more difficult, given the rapid technological innovation in such areas as remote sensing and the greatly enhanced capabilities of future computer hard- and software.

In the counterterrorism arena there have also been impressive advances. While there will be continued major challenges, as noted earlier, in regard to transforming traditional intelligence to meet the threat of seamless terrorism both in the United States and overseas, the counterterrorist community has shared information based on its failures and successes. We have come a long way from the failed attempt to rescue the Israeli hostages in Munich and the abortive Iranian rescue attempt. Such groups as the German GSG 9, the US Delta Forces, the UK's SAS and the Israeli and Jordanian Counterterrorist units have been and will be successful in the inherently dangerous world of counterterrorist operations where success or failure can be measured by a miscalculation of seconds or feet.[6]

Perhaps even more heartening on the analytical and operational level is the fact that despite bureaucratic inertia we can now see that those involved in countering terrorism are developing the counterterrorism networks that have been used so successfully by contemporary terrorists who have practiced their own forms of "netwar." Governments individually and collectively are creating their own flat – as contrasted to traditional ladder – hierarchies that can enable their military, police and intelligence organizations to have their own counterterrorist cadres. Such smaller organizations without a complex bureaucracy can ideally achieve the necessary unity of action and flexibility to seize the initiative, instead of primarily reacting to threats and acts of terrorism. But, again, as in the case of technology there will continue to be a problem of reconciliation. That is, how will governments give the cadre the necessary independence to carry out their actions, while still holding them legally accountable if they engage in criminal activities in the pursuit of their objectives?[7]

Conclusion

Despite the advances in countering terrorism it must always be recognized that it is just as impossible to guarantee personal and collective security from ordinary crime or terrorism. Perhaps it could but the cost of such efforts would make us prisoners in the name of security to governments that would make violations of freedom as illustrated in George Orwell's *1984* rudimentary. It is a risk we dare not take, for by then through our own auto-terrorism and a quest for safety will have created the conditions for terrorism on a scale far greater than imagined by the terrorists of today. Thus in the final analysis by understanding the nature of the threat, placing it in context, taking appropriate actions and working to educate and formulate appropriate policies, we will not eliminate terrorism, but we can learn to take the initiative against those who believe ultimately in a perverted sense of law – that is, we are guilty by location, subject to terrorism by being at the wrong place at the wrong time. Knowledge does mean power in the battle against terrorism.

−7−

Future Terrorism

Predicting the future is perhaps best left to seers, given the track record of many futurologists to assess short-term, much less long-term, trends. But such assessments are of course necessary in any number of fields where policy-makers and leaders in the public and private sectors must not only respond to new events, but also take the initiative, in essence shaping the future. Clearly this necessity to evolve longer-term proactive policies based on effective prediction is especially necessary in regard to the longer-term changes in the evolution of terrorism since, with the development of weapons of mass destruction, the stakes for anticipating and preventing such tragedies as 9/11 have been raised. The fact is, despite the growing ability of governments to respond to acts of terrorism through a whole spectrum of different techniques, including emergency management, crisis management, consequence management and disaster relief, there is recognition that even with the best capabilities and intentions both governments and the public would quickly be overwhelmed by catastrophes resulting from mass terrorism. Moreover, it does not even take an act of mass terrorism to severely disrupt a country or a region even if there are not great physical and human casualties. One only has to look at how the anthrax scare that killed five people closed down the House of Representatives in the United States. Moreover, the case of the Washington, DC, snipers – who were not political terrorists – who were able to terrorize not only people who lived in Washington, but also those in the surrounding region. What would have happened if they'd had a political agenda or belonged to a terrorist organization that engaged in a systematic campaign of terrorism?

The problem of predicting future terrorism is compounded by the fact that one is dealing with those who often belong to or are guided by secret organizations that can range in size from very small compartmentalized cells, where one cell does not know the members of another cell, to larger groups which, in effect, can be viewed as a secret army. Moreover, the terrorists, since they are often engaging in a war against all, have a constellation of targets that cannot be protected by the authorities unless the public is willing to accept the resort to draconian security measures which not only can destroy civil liberties and the right to privacy, but indeed can lead to a form of state terrorism. Moreover, even if such measures were effected, there is no way to have total security against a highly skillful and dedicated adversary. If there is what Clausewitz called "the fog of war," one can suggest that there is an even more dense smog of terrorism. But, the need to forecast is vital or else nations, the public and individuals will face the prospect of living in great uncertainty and will be faced with the shock of reacting to the latest act of carnage and the real or imagined perception that the government cannot provide security for its citizens. And it is worth restating one of the purposes of this book – to help lessen the fear of terrorism that is intensified by what we don't know, in regard to not only modern but also future terrorism.

The analytical framework employed in this chapter has been used in an earlier assessment of future threats to the United States, but this assessment will be far broader and long-term. It will consist of the following interrelated components, some of which were briefly discussed in chapter 2:

- major changes in the international environment and its impact on the motivation of Terrorists
- technological and informational change and consequently innovation in terrorist tactics and strategies
- changes in terrorist's motivation and goals

This transformation of terrorism may point to the future threats we all will have to face.

The International Environment

As noted in chapter 2, the international environment is being buffeted by two often contradictory forces as a result of the impact of globalization. On the one hand, the profound impact of the technological/informational revolution has increased the degree of interdependence at all levels of political, social and economic life. An idealized sense of self-sufficiency within an idealized community – if it ever existed – has been replaced by an often reluctant awareness that parochialism reinforced by old traditions is eroding. Yet, it is that very process of erosion that has led to the assertion of traditional loyalties whether they are based on ethnicity, language, religion or other factors that create real or perceived differences from one group to another.

This reassertion is in part a manifestation of the search for community, a community that as noted before can be smaller than or larger than the boundaries of a nation-state or a geographic region. It is not only a physical quest for community but, equally important, a psychological quest that can generate a sense of loyalty to a homeland thousands of miles from where individuals live or a community that only existed as an ideal based on a unique interpretation of history. The reassertion is also the result of the impact of the very disorderly process of modernization, especially the disruption created by the advent of new demands from industrial, postindustrial and secular states that threaten deeply held beliefs.

One can anticipate that this quest for the reassertion of beliefs will be seen not only in the traditional societies but also in their secular counterparts, where the call for different forms of multiculturalism intensified by shifts in populations through immigration will continue. In many instances, the tensions that will result may be resolved through the forces of assimilation; however, through governmental miscalculation, on the one hand and the frustration of members of a community who believe their identity is not being recognized or even that it is threatened, on the other hand, such tensions can lead to political extremism and ultimately terrorism. The quest for a sense of community in an increasingly interdependent universe – as a means of achieving a degree of psychological and indeed physical security – can ultimately lead to conditions that will create and perpetuate many forms of political violence and specifically the resort to terrorism.

The quest for community has taken on a powerful transcendental quality – as the desire to reassert traditional values and especially beliefs has taken place – with the emergence of religious and especially Islamic fundamentalism. The community in question not only goes beyond borders but includes a vision beyond life. Thus, to the suicide bomber his or her act will ensure entrance to paradise as a martyr. As a result, among these "true believers" who practice their own form of ultimate terrorism and among a broader membership who engage in other forms of violence or support and finance such actions, the resort to terrorism is a religious obligation. Now there are no concerns about acquiring sympathy from nonbelievers or concerns over the overreaction by governments being justified as a result of the acts of terrorism. Without these constraints the contemporary terrorists are now more than willing to use weapons of mass destruction and are unfortunately acquiring the capabilities to do so. What is also vexing is the fact that in this new century other religious fundamentalist may pursue similar destructive paths as part of their own vision. Furthermore it is unfortunately possible that we will see the rise of new cults who will follow the example of Aum Shinrikyo who used sarin gas in the Tokyo subway system as a means of attempting to achieve their goal of literally destroying the existing order.

There will be other groups who may be equally dangerous, even if they are not motivated by their beliefs that they can use terrorism as an expression of their higher morality. As noted earlier, we have seen the reemergence of non-state actors who are challenging the primacy of the nation-state. These non-state actors will include not only members of private armies and security forces, but apolitical terrorists who will hire themselves out as the new mercenaries in the pursuit of their own goals and in conjunction with the numerous new groups which now are a manifestation of the globalization of crime where the old Mafia and the Russian variant will be challenged by other forces using terrorism to engage in highly lucrative worldwide extortion.

Technological Innovations: Netwar, Franchising Terrorism and the Rise of Virtual Terrorism

Perhaps the most significant change in the landscape of terrorism will be the emergence of what may be a fundamental transformation in terrorism as a result of the information revolution – the rise of netwar:

> an emerging mode of conflict (and crime) at societal levels, short of traditional military warfare, in which the protagonists use network forms of organization and related doctrines, strategies and techniques attuned to the information age. These protagonists are likely to consist of dispersed organizations, small groups and individuals who communicate, coordinate and conduct their campaigns in an internetted manner, often without a precise central control. This netwar differs from modes of conflict and crime in which the protagonists prefer to develop formal, stand-alone hierarchical organizations, doctrines and past strategies.[1]

While the murderous evolution of terrorism will continue as traditional operational methods continue to be refined with murderous efficiency, netwar may be opening up a new chapter in the history of terrorism for the following reasons.

In the first place, netwar has enabled terrorists to maintain and increase their security while planning individual acts and campaigns of terrorism. Before the development of the internet, terrorists operated in small compartmentalized cells where the individuals in one cell would not know those in another. This type of organization made it very difficult for authorities to penetrate, especially when the terrorists came from the same family or region. Moreover, the compartmentalization enabled cells to survive if one of their counterparts was exposed and arrested. On the other hand, such compartmentalization made it very difficult for the terrorist organizations to be able to communicate among the cells to launch operations. Therefore emphasis was placed on the local cell taking the initiative in conducting the operations. This initiative had a potentially negative impact for the cell and the organization it belonged to, because local initiative remote from central control could lead to factionalization and instability of a higher command to exercise its authority.

But with the coming of the internet this changed. The terrorists could maintain their security through the cell-like structure but also conduct operations with other cells without compromising their identity or location since such communication took place in the anonymity of cyberspace. Even with sophisticated computers it is hard to track various groups through the electronic babble where it is increasingly difficult to "separate the noise from the signal." Furthermore, terrorists now have at their disposal cryptographic capabilities that rival those of the intelligence services attempting to electronically penetrate their messages. In effect the internet has created another layer of clandestineness for terrorist cells and organizations, making them even more difficult to expose.

In the second place, the organizational design of netwar has placed and will continue to place a heavy burden on traditional bureaucracies and their organizational formats for combating terrorists. Traditional bureaucracies rely on a pyramid, top-down, hierarchical structure. Decisions flow from the top down with many layers between the senior executives and the individuals in the field. Furthermore, there is often competition with other organizations and within organizations, even if there are common goals. One organization with its own "stove pipe" might not share information or coordinate with its counterparts – such a failure is well documented in the report produced by the commission charged with detailing what happened on 9/11 and other publications.[2]

In contrast, terrorists, by now having the ability to maintain their security through their cell-like organizations but to coordinate activities via the internet, have a much more flexible approach in seeking their goals. The terrorists at the local level do not have to deal with the slow process of decision-making that are the mark of contemporary bureaucracies. They can act independently. Moreover, using Al Qaeda as a prototype, contemporary terrorists now are involved in their own form of deadly franchise. Each of their groups has a stand-alone capability but can acquire technical, financial and operational support from a larger network.

Finally and perhaps most unfortunately, today's terrorists, despite their own diversity based on religion, location, ethnicity and other factors, have achieved a degree of unity yet to be mirrored in the operation of counterterrorism organizations in individual countries, much less on the regional and international level. This does not mean to suggest that progress has not been made. But in this age of Weapons of Mass destruction, the clock is ticking.

The Emergence of Virtual Terrorism

Perhaps the most disturbing thing, in reference to potential future trends, may be the ability and willingness of terrorists to alter and magnify their threat capabilities by altering the perception of the people watching through use of the Internet and other forms of modern communication. The alteration process has already, in the form of more effective staging of terrorist incidents, seized the world's visual headlines. Certainly the terrorists' "spectaculars" are not as new as the seizure of three jet aircraft in 1970 that led to the civil war in Jordan, the Munich massacre in 1972 and the ability of the Iranian government to effectively capture the US media in 1979 for more than 444 days. The birth of *America Held Hostage*, the name of an evening program that ultimately became known as *Nightline*, occurred to bring nightly updates of the hostage situation. The tradition continues both in campaigns and individual acts of terrorism. The car bombings in Iraq fill the news each evening and the chilling sights of captured hostages whose decapitations have been shown on television have opened up an new age of terrorist voyeurs.

What is especially vexing, however, is the fact that – particularly through the use of the Internet – terrorists do not necessarily have to stage violent acts to gain attention. They will use the web as a means of conveying their message even without the resort to physical violence. A bellwether for this trend took place when the well-respected former Press Secretary for President Kennedy, the late Pierre Salinger, announced that it was missiles that destroyed a TWA jet in 1996. He later admitted that he received the information through unverified Internet reporting. The damage was done and the notion of "shelf life" based on conspiracy theories implicating the US Navy or terrorists was initiated. In effect, the terrorists did not even have to engage in any operations or take credit in order to instill fear by altering perception not based on fact but on the often very questionable sources on the World Wide Web.

One can anticipate that in the future the terrorists will create their own internet-driven plots complete with false attacks and the generation of conspiracies and attendant public fear without having to resort directly to violence, for they will be engaging in virtual terrorism – a form of information warfare that alters the public's perception of a threat without the physical resort to violence.

To compound matters, governments have intentionally or unintentionally engaged in auto-terrorism by scaring the public through warning of potential terrorist actions without providing necessary information, within the limits of protecting sensitive information or suggesting what actions the public should take on "actionable intelligence" to deal with the threat. The problem of finding a way of increasing awareness without creating paranoia is a difficult task; for example, the US color-coded system, which is now being changed, probably created more fear or, at best, placed people in a mental state such that they would ignore the warnings. The danger of "crying wolf" or "the sky is falling" goes beyond children's tales.

Conclusion

In the long run, the basic goal of instilling fear in the public as a means of dramatizing causes and attempting to achieve political change will continue to be a hallmark of terrorism and there will be continuity through the resort to bombings, hostage taking and other traditional forms of terrorism. The change in motivation, fueled by fundamentalism, the availability of new weapons and the use of the information revolution to alter perception of the threat of terrorism, will be magnified in the years to come. It is time for bureaucracies, not known for their ability to be creative, to start winning the war of innovation and imagination against very creative and resourceful adversaries. It cannot be "business as usual" – underreaction followed by overreaction – after an incident in the protracted conflict known as terrorism.

Appendix

Working through Terrorism at the Individual, Family and Community Levels

J.B. Hill and Joshua A. Smith

Understanding and preparedness are the hallmarks of fear reduction. To understand is to eliminate the unknown and allow people to act in the face of something they fear. To prepare is to acquire the knowledge that you have a plan even in a time of crisis. It is important that we remember that terrorists are individuals who have made their decisions – no matter how terrible they may seem – along rational and coherent lines. Knowing this will allow people to make decisions that can not only make their lives easier in times of great tension, but also perhaps even save those lives.

The purpose of this appendix is to give the readers a guide for working through the difficult concepts of terrorism and help them formulate a plan on what to do in any type of emergency, but more specifically during and after an act of terrorism. After the readers understand it, they can then take the curriculum to friends, families and communities to facilitate discussion through which terrorism can be talked about freely, in order to reduce fear in reacting and responding to terrorist events. Through understanding what terrorism is and is not, one can be mentally prepared to deal with acts of terrorism more easily and logically, rather than with a primal, emotional reaction. It is meant to apply to all: both primary victims – those who are directly affected by the act of terrorism – and secondary victims – those who are victimized through having watched an attack take place via media sources.

While parts of the appendix may seem repetitive to those who have read the book, it should be recalled that there are many who have not done so and can still benefit from the information. Thus, the appendix in some ways is a concise version of the book, as both have the same goal – fear reduction. The appendix, however, is meant to be used either in conjunction with or apart from the book, to help those who have not read it in its entirety to understand terrorism and how to prepare for it.

Keeping this purpose in mind, the appendix is broken into four main sections:

- Placing terrorism in context
- How to cope with terrorism at various levels
- Preparedness
- A guided series of questions to facilitate discussion

Placing Terrorism in Context

While many have attempted to define terrorism, no firm definition has ever been agreed upon. The League of Nations Convention in 1937 defined terrorism as "all criminal acts directed against a State and intended or calculated to create a state of terror in the minds of particular persons." A short legal definition proposed to the United Nations Crime Branch by A.P. Schmid was "act of terrorism = peacetime equivalent of war crime."[1] The US Department of State defines terrorism as "premeditated, politically motivated violence perpetrated against noncombatant targets by subnational groups or clandestine agents, usually intended to influence an audience."[2] Obviously no one is expected to memorize these definitions, but there are some characteristics that many scholars agree are applied to terrorism and knowing some of these can help put terrorism in the context of real world experience.

Terrorism is a purposeful act that is almost always political in nature. It is not a phenomenon that originated in the twentieth century. It has been around for at least hundreds, if not thousands, of years and has been carried out in many different forms and fashions.

Attacks can be carried out by an individual or a group. An attack may take many forms – anything from a bombing to a kidnapping – but it almost always involves violence. It is not a random event and not often is it carried out by someone who is crazy or considered "deranged." This separates terrorism from everyday crime, despite crimes often involving terrorizing people. A crime may cause terror, but it is not necessarily terrorism.

During the times immediately following an attack, the term "terrorism" is thrown about with reckless abandon. This only helps to improve the depth, scope and impact of the attack. It is important to understand that with terrorism fear is the weapon, not the bomb or kidnapping – these are just some of the instruments used by terrorists. Terrorist attacks are directed at three different adversaries. First, there is the target – the government or state-sponsored organization which the terrorist group is fighting to change (or destroy). Second, there is the victim (also known as primary victim, direct victim or first-order victim) – the person or persons who are wounded and/or killed by the violence of the attack. Finally and most importantly, there is the audience (also known as the secondary victim, indirect victim or second-order victim). The size of the audience affected by the attack is the real measure of success for terrorists.

The purpose of any terrorist attack is to cause fear in those witnessing the act. Because of this, terrorism is a potent form of psychological warfare. Fear is the primary response terrorists are looking for because fear can paralyze a community or an entire nation. Fear often lingers after the initial attack. The constant TV replay of attacks, the unending headlines by the print media, cause a rippling effect on the pool of fear. A continuous cycle of visual violence takes place. With every replay and with every headline, another group of viewers become victims. The moment people view an act of terrorism through an outlet of the media and find themselves emotionally involved, they become secondary victims of the attack. With today's worldwide access to media, most people can and have, become secondary victims of a terrorist attack.

Unfortunately, many people simply do not understand that their emotional reaction caused by fear of attack is exactly what the terrorists want. Fear encourages and feeds the motivation behind the attacks. That is why it is so important for everyone to understand exactly what terrorism is and is not. Through this understanding, people can learn to not react on the primal, emotional level, but rather to work with a logical analysis of what is going on and what needs to be done to get through the situation.

How to Cope with Terrorism at Various Levels

Individual

On the individual level there are two ways you can be victimized by terrorism. The first is by becoming a first-order victim – one who is directly involved in the attack itself. This could be through means of kidnapping, bombing or any other tactic used by a terrorist. The second way is by becoming a second-order victim – one who is indirectly involved in the attack. This could mean that you either witnessed the attack (in person or via a media source) or know someone who was killed, injured or taken hostage during the event. Primary victims almost always require some type of medical treatment immediately following an attack.

It should be mentioned that there is still some debate as to the designation of first- and second-order victims. Some professionals believe that the first-order victim is actually the audience, while those attacked are second-order. This curriculum will utilize the first descriptions mentioned above.

No matter what the circumstances, if one is involved in a terrorist attack, that person should consider psychological assistance. The accumulation of the stress that an attack can bring over a long period of time can cause unpleasant and unhealthy reactions. Seeking help from a professional counselor can reduce the possibility of such byproducts of terrorism. It is important that you face the realities of what terrorism is when putting it in context and quite often it is a frightening situation. Remember that you should not let fear control your reactions. In any terrorist incident, you will benefit most by being able to react logically.

Family

Spending time with your family after a terrorist attack can be a great source of comfort while trying to cope with what has just happened. Having a loved one attacked or kidnapped can be profoundly damaging emotionally. Clearly, there are differences between first- and second-order victims. Despite these differences, many of the stages and their coping methods are applicable to both the family and the victim. Having faith in the rescue attempt and taking one day at a time are essential if families are to retain what is most important in dealing with any terrorist attack – keeping hope alive. Communication between members of the family not affected by the attack is also an essential form of coping.

Community

Dealing with a terrorist attack as a community can be a very difficult challenge. Attacks are felt by individuals and families on a personal level, while a community has to deal with not only the loss of its members, but possibly the loss of critical infrastructure. In many ways, crisis management during a terrorist attack, is "panic management." Managing panic in even a small community can be difficult. With events such as 9/11 and the train bombings in Madrid, it can develop into riot, causing even more fear, panic and disorientation.

One of the community's primary responsibilities is making sure resources are available to those who need them. This includes everything from first responders being able to reach the incident to immediate professional counseling for members of the community who are affected by the incident. Just as communities have crisis-management plans for severe storms, similar crisis-management techniques and planning can be employed to handle terrorist situations.

It might be difficult for the populace to believe than "an attack happened here." They might feel as if their world has been altered and that they have lost control. While many of the levels of coping are similar to those for the individual and family, it must be kept in mind that they are not equivalents. Communities have much more to respond to; not the least of which is anger – caused by profiling or stereotyping – directed toward a specific group of people who may share the same ethnicity or religious beliefs as those responsible for the attack. This can cause violence of another type to erupt and must be kept in check and dealt with quickly. Everyone must avoid the dangers of rushing to judgment, stereotyping and seeking an enemy.

Communities often find themselves in turmoil following an attack. Confusion can lead to further injuries and prevent those who need immediate assistance from receiving it. Crisis-management planning is the most important thing a community can engage in to help thwart the byproducts of a terrorist attack. As mentioned before, techniques used for dealing with severe storms and other natural disasters can be effective when producing plans to handle terrorist attacks, but it is possible for such plans to fall apart during an attack. Thus, it is important that emergency plans are tested as thoroughly as possible with alternatives ready in the event that key resources are damaged.

Preparedness

Individual/Family Planning

Have a communication plan that allows family members or even just an individual, to contact others within the family and outside of the area to let people know they are all right.

● It may be easier to make long-distance calls, so it is important that you have an out-of-town contact to keep family members in touch with each other.

- Be sure everyone knows the number and has a way to make the call (e.g. calling card, mobile phone, email, etc.).

Have plans for both staying put and leaving.

- Plans for staying put can include things like a disaster preparedness kit. A family should plan on one gallon of water per person per day for drinking and sanitation. (Children, nursing mothers and sick people may require more.) You should also store at least a three-day supply of food. (You'll find that you might already have this in nonperishables.) Make sure the foods don't require refrigeration, preparation or cooking and don't require much water. Make sure you have eating utensils and a manual can-opener.
- Plans for leaving must include maps of the area in which you will be traveling (this ties in to making sure you have a location to get to) and extra gas if you're traveling by car. Plans should not count on public transportation being accessible. If you must split up with family members, make sure you have a way to contact them in case of a second emergency.

Travel.

- Depending on where and when you are traveling, it is possible that travel times are the most dangerous in terms of terrorism. This can be because of lack of knowledge of an area or how to get home in an emergency. Thus, travel requires special preparation.

   First, make sure you know the threats before you leave for the country. The US government has excellent resources for this, including the *CIA World Factbook*. Checking news about the area online is also very helpful. Travel advice is also available from the British government, which compiles a list of advice from other countries at the Foreign & Commonwealth Office website <http://www.fco.gov.uk>.

Then, once you're in the country, make sure you have ID with you and make sure the embassy knows that you're there. Usually this occurs naturally if you have to apply for a visa to the country you're visiting, but if you do not need one, make sure to contact the embassy nevertheless. If any type of terrorist event occurs, make sure you have the embassy phone number and can call to ask what to do. Also try to line up transportation to the embassy in case it is required.

Determine if your family's schools and places of employment have emergency plans.

- Ask how they will keep in contact with families during an emergency.
- If anyone in your family has special needs, make sure schools and places of employment have supplies available to meet those needs.

Community Planning

Communicate with neighbors.

- Determine if anyone has special supplies or skills such as power generators and medical experience.
- Have a place for children to go in the event their families have not made it home.

Make sure your community has a crisis management plan that deals with terrorist attacks.

- Designing a crisis-management plan is beyond the scope of this appendix, but if you're interested in gathering more information, in the United States you can contact the Department of Homeland Security. Citizens of other countries can contact their respective agency that deals with homeland security. In the UK a relevant site is <http://londonprepared.gov.uk/ antiterrorism>.

Planning as an *individual* is relatively simple. One must know where to go, how to get in contact with others and where to seek physical and medical assistance if necessary. Courses in CPR and other first-responder techniques can be significantly helpful in an emergency. On all levels, knowledge is the most useful tool for preparation. Knowing your surroundings and any possible threats can help you steer clear of being involved in an attack to begin with. Terrorism awareness is a vital function that can help to prevent an act from taking place. If you know what you're looking for, you will be more likely to notice any strange or unusual events that could be preparation for an attack. It is very important to keep vigilant, but not let your imagination or paranoia get the best of you. If you have carefully analyzed the situation and you feel there is a credible threat, do not hesitate to notify the local authorities of your concern.

Planning on the *family* level is slightly more complicated. The most important thing is to define the lines of communication. Keep in mind that following any disaster, cell phones have a tendency to lose their signal or become so jammed with calls that nothing gets through. Sometimes land lines are also too busy. Because of this, it can be very helpful to have a central location where everyone can meet. Also, a contact person outside of your local area can some-times be more accessible via phone. Each family member should call this person to let him or her know they are okay. The contact can then report to the other members of the family as they call in. Through this intermediary, contact with your family can be main-tained.

Families should also have a mini-emergency plan. A backup location to meet is very important so the family can reunite in the event their primary location wasn't accessible. The proper things to do in an emergency should be discussed as a family. Getting away from the area of the incident should be a top priority for all members of the family. There are several practical reasons for this, not the least of which is to avoid a second attack. Terrorists will often have a second wave of attack to hurt first responders trying to assist those hurt in the first wave. More important, however, is the fact that no matter the rationale for staying, there is a good chance that any civilians present might interfere with the work of those first responders. Another important topic to discuss as a family is what to do if a member of the family is missing. This is a difficult topic to discuss, but it is very important. It is especially important to emphasize that *all* members of the family should be involved with this discussion. Age does not disqualify someone from being involved in an attack. While a discussion of possible emergencies may be frightening to them, it is good for children to see that the adults are prepared. Also, do not underestimate the creativity of children in assisting with the plans. Frequently, they think of things that adults wouldn't even consider.

It is important for every *community* to recognize its threat level. For most communities it is relatively low, but for no community should it be considered non-existent. Population and major transportation hubs have a lot to do with a community's threat level, but it cannot be generalized and it cannot be perfectly judged. Each individual community must realistically assess its threat level and do its best to plan accordingly.

The first area of concentration is crisis management. Most communities have some type of crisis-management plan in place. These can be important starting points for planning how to deal with a terrorist attack. Understanding what areas of your community are best prepared can help strengthen other areas. It is important to recognize some differences between plans for natural disasters and those for terrorist attacks. Both require the assistance of police, firefighters and emergency medical teams. Also, a good plan will keep the mental health of its community in mind. If at all possible, professional counselors should be made available for anyone who feels the need for treatment of psychological stress caused by the attack.

Communities also have the burden of maintaining their critical infrastructure – anything that the city must have in order to operate. During any disaster, this must be kept working smoothly. With small communities it can be relatively simple – something as straightforward as a chain of command can be enough to keep things running without any problems. In larger communities, however, it can be much more difficult. The larger the infrastructure, the larger the possibility of it failing – community leaders must keep this in mind when creating a crisis-management plan. Alternatives must be considered: this is where creativity and imagination are most useful.

Identifying critical, informal leaders within a community is essential for both passing on information and maintaining order. Conduits of information between the formal leadership and the citizens of the community can sometimes be convoluted. The inclusion of informal community leaders in the crisis-management plan offers a bridge that makes information more accessible. It can also assist in the flow of information from citizens to the formal leadership. People in larger communities have a tendency to trust their local leaders more than leaders higher up on the ladder whom they don't know.

Ideally, no individual, family or community would have to deal with terrorism. In reality, however, terrorism will affect all of us in one way or another. If we manage to be prepared, we can reduce the cost it can have on our life. If not, we risk everything.

Questions to Facilitate Discussion

Finally, here are some questions to help foster conversation among your family, friends and community. There are not any right or wrong answers and the idea is not to argue points of contention. Rather, these questions are meant to help those involved better understand terrorism, how to prepare for it and what to do if they are involved in a terrorist attack.

1. What is terrorism and how do we know?

2. Who is a potential target for terrorists? What increases the likelihood of being a target?
3. Why do you need more than crisis management to combat the effects of a terrorist attack?
4. What are some general concepts of crisis management dealing with terrorist events at the community level?
5. Within a family, what are techniques you can use to make sure your family stays in contact with each other in the event of a crisis?
6. Why is having an emergency plan so important?
7. What are some ways for an individual to plan for a terrorist attack? Are these options applicable to all individuals?
8. If I am affected by a terrorist event, what should I do and what are some *incorrect* ways to react? Why are these reactions incorrect?

Conclusion

Please keep in mind that this curriculum is meant to facilitate fear reduction. Through the information in this appendix and the discussions that come from the preceding questions, we hope that you have learned what terrorism is and understand that the main purpose of it is to instill fear. We also hope that you now have some idea of how to prepare for a terrorist event.

You are meant to share this information with your family and community. Please do so. Understanding is the hallmark of fear reduction and reducing fear has an immediate effect on the power terrorists hold over you, your family and your community.

Notes

Introduction: Imagery and Reality

1. Brian Jenkins, *International Terrorism: A New Mode of Conflict*, California Seminar on Arms Control and Foreign Policy Research Paper No. 48 (Los Angeles: Crescent, 1975), p. 2.

2. Sun Tzu, *The Art of War*.

1 The Meaning of Terrorism: Cutting through the Semantic Jungle

1. For an extensive discussion of different definitions based on interviews with the leading specialists, see "Terrorism and Related Concepts," chapter 1 in Alex P. Schmid and Albert J. Jongman, *Political Terrorism: A New Guide to Actors, Authors, Concepts, Data Bases, Theories and Literature* (Amsterdam: SWIDOC, 1998).

2. Hannah Arendt, *Eichman in Jerusalem: Report on the Banality of Evil* (New York: Penguin, 1977).

3. Eric Hoffer, *The True Believer: Thoughts on the Nature of Mass Movements* (New York: HarperCollins, 1989).

4. David Lyon, *Surveillance Society: Monitoring Everyday Life* (New York: McGraw-Hill, 2001).

5. National Advisory Committee on Criminal Justice, Standards and Goals, *Disorders and Terrorism: Report on the Task Force on Disorders and Terrorism* (Washington, DC: US Government Printing Office, 1978), p. 3.

6. George Orwell, *Nineteen Eighty-Four* (London: Everyman, 1984).

7. Bruce Hoffman, *Inside Terrorism* (New York: Columbia University Press, 1998), p. 43.

8. Armir Tahiri, *Holy Terror: The Inside Story on Islamic Terrorism* (London: Sphere, 1987).

9. For an extensive discussion of asymmetric warfare, see Colonel Lloyd J. Matthews, *Challenging the United States Symmetrically and Asymmetrically: Can America be Defeated?* (Carlisle Barracks, PA: US Army War College, Strategic Studies Institute, 1998).

10. Robert Tabert, *The War of the Flea: A Study of Guerrilla Warfare* (New York: Lyle Stewart, 1965).

11. Stephen Sloan, *The Anatomy of Non-Territorial Terrorism: An Analytical Essay* (Gaithersburg, MD: International Association of Chiefs of Police, 1978), p. 3.

12. For an excellent study on the privatization of warfare and security, see P.W. Singer, *Corporate Warriors: The Rise of the Privatized Military Industry* (Ithaca: Cornell University Press, 2003).

13. From conversation between the author and John O'Neill. John was a remarkable man whose dedication to countering terrorism was legendary. He had continually to fight a bureaucracy whose inertia and lack of imagination stood in the way of effectively combating terrorism. Tragically, he died on 9/11 at the World Trade Center, where he had just started his new position as Chief of Security. See Murray Weiss, *The Man Who Warned America: The Life and Death of John O'Neill, the FBI's Embattled Counterterror Warrior* (New York: Regan Books, 2003).

14. For an excellent discussion of the different types of doctrine, see Dennis M. Drew, "Of Trees and Leaves: A New View of Doctrine," *Air University Review,* January/February, 1982.

2 Terrorism: A Historical Perspective

1. For a classic, exhaustive study of the strategy, tactics and practice of guerrilla warfare, see Robert Asprey, *War in the Shadows* (Garden City, NY: Doubleday, 1975).

2. For a discussion of historical and contemporary terrorist groups, see Sean Kendal Andersen and Stephen Sloan, *Terrorism: Assassins to Zealots* (Lanham, MD: Scarecrow Press, 2003). This paperback is a revised edition of *The Historical Dictionary of Terrorism*, 2nd edn, 2002.

3. Rupert Emerson, *From Empire to Nation: The Rise to Self-Assertion of Asian and African People* (Cambridge, MA: Harvard University Press, 1960), pp. 95–6.

4. Maurice A. East, "The International System Perspective and Foreign Policy," in Maurice A. East et al. (eds), *Why Nations Act: A Theoretical Perspective for Comparative Foreign Policy Studies* (Beverly Hills, CA: Sage Publications, 1978), p. 145.

5. Stephen Sloan, "Technology and Terrorism: Privatizing Public Violence," *IEEE Technology and Society Magazine*, Summer 1991.

6. Xavier Raufer, "Gray Areas: A New Security Threat," *Political Warfare: Intelligence, Active Measures and Terrorism Report*, Spring 1992, p.1.

3 The Rationale of Terror

1. The Japanese Red Army embraced a mixture of left-wing ideology with their own mystical interpretation for their unique goal to ferment a global revolution. It is very difficult to character-ize them, for their goals transcended the traditional justifications that have been used by terrorists. While the JRA legacy goes back to the Japanese student radicalism in the 1960s, the organization changed into a cult where extremist ideology did not retain as deeply held beliefs. The "army" (in name only) increasingly acted as a cult and its members turned on each other. For an outstanding book on this most interesting and disturbing group, see William R Farrell, *Blood and Race: The Story of the Japanese Red Army* (Lexington, MA: Lexington Books, 1990).

2. Carlos Marighella, *The Mini-Manual of the Urban Guerrilla*, trans. Gene Z. Hanrahan (Chapel Hill, NC: Documentary Books, 1985).

3. I had the distinct pleasure and honor of appearing with Sir Geoffrey Jackson on a British television show. Even in that short time his warmth, charm and dignity were readily apparent. His book, *Surviving the Long Night* should be required reading for those diplomats and businesspeople who may go into harm's way. Jackson illustrates how, despite the profound psychological pressures of captivity, one can survive with honor and dignity. Geoffrey Jackson, *Surviving the Long Night: An Autobiographical Account of a Political Kidnapping* (New York: Vanguard, 1974).

4. Thirty-seven years after the bombing, one of the perpetrators, Thomas Blanton, a former member of the Ku Klux Klan, was found guilty and sentenced to life imprisonment. While justice was delayed, it did take place and the verdict sent a message. If terrorism is a form of protracted war, so can law-enforcement agents maintain the search for justice long after the incident.

4   The Strategies and Tactics of Terrorism

1. Sergei Nechaev, "Revolutionary Catechism," in F. Venturi, *Roots of Revolutions: A History of Populist and Socialist Movements in Nineteenth Century Russia*, trans. F. Haskell (London: International Institute for Strategic Studies, 1966), p. 281.

2. Richard E. Rubenstein, "Revolutionary Terror: the Anarcho-Communists," in his *Alchemists of a Revolution: Terrorism in the Modern World* (New York: Basic Books, 1987).

3. "Baader-Meinhof Manifesto," trans. Robert Rynerson, <http://www.baader-meinhof.com/students/resources/internetlink/index.htm> – linked to: <http://home.att.net/~rw.rynerson/rafgrund.htm>

4. Bruce Hoffman, *Inside Terrorism* (New York: Columbia University Press, 1999), p. 18.

5. David E. Kaplan and Andrew Marshall, *The Cult at the End of the World* (New York: Crown Publishers, 1986), p. 16.

6. In a very debatable move, both the *New York Times* and the *Washington Post* published the 30,500-word manifesto on June 19, 1995 because the Unabomber said he would cease attacks. It was

also done at the request of Attorney General Janet Reno who, on the advice of the Federal Bureau of Investigation, thought the style and content would help lead to the Unabomber's apprehension. The Unabomber, Ted Kaczynski, is now serving a life sentence.

7. From Hamas' website <http://www.hamasonline.com/>

8. Rohan Gunaratna, *Inside Al Qaeda: Global Network of Terrorism* (New York: Columbia University Press, 2002), p. 89.

9. *The Army of God: The Declaration*: <http://www.armyofgod. org/>

10. This communiqué was posted on the Internet. A copy of it can be found at <http://www.iiipublishing.com/elf.htm> and more information can be found about the Earth Liberation Front at http://www.earthliberationfront.com/

11. William Powell, *The Anarchist Cookbook* (New York: Lyle Stuart, 1970). For an example of the current level of instruction on tactics, see *The Al Qaeda Manual*, United States Department of Justice <http://www.usdoj.gov/ag/trainingmanual.htm>. The manual was on a computer seized in the home of an Al Qaeda member by the Manchester Metropolitan Police in the United Kingdom. The Department of Justice felt that its dissemination would help law enforcement agencies understand and counter terrorist tactics. Unfortunately, there are others who can utilize the manual in other, less warranted, means. The classic challenge of freedom of information and need-to-know is aptly illustrated by this case.

5   The Attack and its Enduring Legacy: The Psychological Impact of Terrorism

1. Douglas S. Derrer, "Crisis Stages and Hostage Survival," in his *We Are All Targets: A Handbook of Terrorism Avoidance and Hostage Survival* (Annapolis, MD: Naval Institute Press, 1992) pp. 33–55.

2. Geoffrey Jackson, *Surviving the Long Night: An Autobiographical Account of a Political Kidnapping* (New York: Vanguard Press, 1974).

3. The concept of "keeping the faith" has been used with impressive results by military personnel who were subject to horrendous treatment as prisoners of war in North Vietnam. I was honored to be able to tape the experience of the late Captain Howard Rutledge when he was Commander of the Naval Reserve Training Corps at the University of Oklahoma. His experience underscores the remarkable ability of individuals not only to survive, but to survive with honor.

4. Dianne Meyers, RN, MSN, *Weapons of Mass Destruction/ Terrorism Orientation Pilot Project*, Clara Barton Center for Domestic Preparedness, Pine Bluff, AR, August 15–17, 2001.

5. Over the years, I have conducted workshops for state and local law-enforcement personnel and first responders on how to prevent, deter and respond to terrorism. Such meetings have been particularly useful when members of the community also attend, because these men and women become directly involved in the challenges of combating terrorism at the local level. The programs of the Idaho Office of Disaster Services have been pioneers of community involvement.

6. As the aesthetic, political, economic and emotional debate over what type of structures and grounds should be used in memoriam of the World Trade Center, some excellent lessons can be drawn from the participation of the survivors and community involved in the Oklahoma City bombing. To appreciate the process, see Edward T. Linenthal, *Preserving Memories* (New York: Columbia University Press, 2001). For a very insightful critique of the selection process of the Oklahoma Memorial, also see <http://www.jamesrobertwatson.com/bombingmemorial.html>.

6. The Policy Dimensions: On the Community, National and International Level

1. The changes in regard to both US domestic and its international security are – and will be in the years to come – greatly significant as Washington addresses how to cope with both traditional and new threats. The Homeland Security Act of 2002 established a

new cabinet-level department that is altering the face of domestic organizational capabilities and policies to address domestic threats and their relationship to those in the international environment.

2. The Intelligence Reform and Prevention of Terrorism Act of 2004 has altered the organizations and roles of the US intelligence community. As in the case of the establishment of the Department of Homeland Security, it remains to be seen whether reorganization, centralization and significant funding will effectively address the continuity and change which characterize terrorism, other forms of political violence and warfare.

3. Steven Strasser, ed., *The 9/11 Investigation: Staff Reports of the 9/11 Commission* (New York: Public Affairs, 2004).

4. I was the main subject-matter/educational consultant for a four-part video series titled *Terrorism in our World* (Wynnewood, PA: Schlesinger Media, a division of Library Video Company. Produced and directed by CBS, 2003). The writers and producers consciously faced the challenges of not sensationalizing the topic and at the same time providing middle and high school students a meaningful context with which to understand terrorism.

5. Paul Wilkinson, *Terrorism and the Liberal State* (New York: John Wiley, 1978). The issues raised in this book are even more important now than they were in 1978 when terrorism was considered by many to be something that happened to other people in other parts of the world.

6. There are many books available on counterterrorist forces; some are quite sensational, others more academic. For a decent overview, see Leroy Thompson, *The Rescuers: The World's Top Anti-Terrorist Units* (Boulder, CO: Paladin Press, 1986).

7. For a discussion of the need for such units and a doctrine of taking the initiative against terrorists, see Stephen Sloan, *Beating International Terrorism: An Action Strategy for Preemption and Punishment* (Montgomery, AL: Air University Press, 2000). The first edition was almost not published, because it was counter to the primarily reactive US counterterrorism policies at that time. It has achieved a degree of official respectability with the passage of time and events.

7 Future Terrorism

1. John Arquilla and David Rondfeldt, eds, *Networks and Netwar: The Future of Terror, Crime and Militancy* (Santa Monica, CA: Rand, 2001), p. 6.

2. If the reader is interested in pursuing his or her understanding of terrorism, the following report is a must read. It not only provides great detail on the circumstances that led up to 9/11, but also suggests what needs to be done to greatly lessen such events. The report has lessons that need to be learned by all governments confronting the reality of terrorism. See Steven Strasser, ed., *The 9/11 Investigation: Staff Reports of the 9/11 Commission* (New York: Public Affairs, 2004).

Appendix

1. United Nations Office on Drugs and Crime, "UNODC – Terrorism Definitions," <http://www.unodc.org/unodc/terrorism_definitions.html>.

2. Title 22 of the United States code, Section 2656f(d).

Further Reading

These books represent some of the best material out there for those who wish to further their knowledge of terrorism. One must be aware that opportunists take advantage of events such as 9/11 and the London bombings, so the material that is read should be chosen carefully. This list is not meant to be exhaustive, just enough to give readers a point from which to begin their studies. It includes both scholarly material and appropriate trade books with a bit of source material. From these texts, and others, readers can gain insight into the world of terrorism, and that insight can aid in fear reduction, which is the goal of this book.

Andersen, Sean K. and Stephen Sloan. 2003. *Terrorism: Assassins to Zealot.* Lanham, MD: Scarecrow Press.

Arquilla, John and David Ronfeldt, eds. 2001. *Networks and Netwar: The Future of Terror, Crime and Militancy.* Santa Monica, CA: Rand Corporation.

Bersia, John C. 2003. *World War 4: Confronting Terrorism.* Orlando, FL: Global Connections Foundation.

Bushnell, P. T., Vladimir Shlapentokh et. al., eds. 1991. *State Organized Terror: The Case of Violent Internal Repression.* Boulder, CO: Westview.

Charters, David and Graham F. Walker, eds. 2004. *After 9/11: Terrorism and Crime in a Globalized World.* Fredericton, N.B.: Centre for Conflict Studies, University of New Brunswick, and Dalhousie, N.S.: Centre for Foreign Policy Studies, Dalhousie University.

Clark, Richard. 2004. *Against All Enemies: Inside America's War on Terrorism.* New York: Free Press.

Gunaratna, Rohan. 2002. *Inside Al Qaeda: Global Network of Terrorism.* New York: Columbia University Press.

Hoffman, Bruce. 1999. *Inside Terrorism.* New York: Columbia University Press.

Howard, Russell D. and Reid L. Sawyer. 2004. *Terrorism and Counterterrorism: Understanding the New Security Environment, Readings and Interpretations, Revised and Updated.* McGraw-Hill.

Juergensmeyer, Mark. 2000. *Terror in the Mind of God: The Global Rise of Religious Terrorism.* Berkeley: University of California Press.

Laqueur, Walter. 2004. *Voices of Terror: Manifestos, Writings and Manuals of Al Qaeda, Hamas, and other Terrorists from around the World and Throughout the Ages.* Naperville, IL: Sourcebooks.

9/11 Commission Report: The Final Report of the National Commission on Terrorist Attacks upon the United States (Authorized Edition). 2004. New York: Norton.

Norris, Pippa, Montague Kern and Marion Just. 2003. *Framing Terrorism: The News Media, the Government, and the Public.* New York: Taylor and Francis.

Reinares, Fernando, ed. 2000. *European Democracies Against Terrorism: Governmental Politics and Intergovernmental Co-operation.* Part of a series by the Onati Institute for the Sociology of Law. Aldershot: Ashgate.

Sageman, Mark. 2004. *Understanding Terror Networks.* Philadelphia: University of Pennsylvania Press.

Shulsky, Abram N. 1993. *Silent Warfare: Understanding the World of Intelligence.* 2nd edn. Revised Gary Schmitt. Washington: Brassey's (US).

Stern, Jessica. 2003. *Terror in the Name of God: Why Religious Militants Kill.* New York: HarperCollins.

Wikinson, Paul. 2000. *Terrorism Versus Democracy: The Liberal State Response.* London: Cass.

Index